THE MAGIC

The Story of a Film

Other Books by Christopher Priest

Novels:

The Separation
The Extremes
The Prestige
The Quiet Woman
The Glamour
The Affirmation
A Dream of Wessex
The Space Machine
Inverted World
Fugue for a Darkening Island
Indoctrinaire

Short story collections:

Ersatz Wines
The Dream Archipelago
An Infinite Summer
Real-Time World

THE MAGIC

The Story of a Film

Christopher Priest

Christopher Priest

Dec '09

GrimGrin
Studio

The Magic

First paperback edition

Published by

GrimGrin Studio
32 Elphinstone Road
Hastings
East Sussex
TN34 2EQ
United Kingdom
grimgrin@gmx.com

Contents

1. The End (part i)

In October 2006 a film based on the novel *The Prestige* opened in the USA. It was launched on 2,281 screens across the nation, and took more than $5 millions on the first day. This immediately placed it at the top of the US box office. At the end of the first full week the film had taken over $19 millions, and by the time it finished its domestic run it had taken more than $53 millions. Subsequently the film has reached a total worldwide income of $103 millions, based on theatrical screenings. (This figure does not include DVD sales and rentals, downloads or television rights.)

On the Internet Movie Database list of the 250 most popular films of all time, *The Prestige* is presently placed in the high 80s, not far beneath *2001: A Space Odyssey*, *Singin' in the Rain* and *Some Like it Hot*. It is a long way ahead of such films as *Kill Bill: Vol. 1* (which is about halfway down the list), *King Kong* (the original from 1933, which is close to the 200 mark) and *La Dolce Vita* (near the bottom). On this list it has consistently shown higher ratings than dozens of other extremely well known films, all regarded as classics of the screen.[1]

Some of the other well-regarded major films released at roughly the same time as *The Prestige* do not appear on this list at all – they include *The Queen*, *The Illusionist*, *Babel* and *The Last King of Scotland*.

On its release on DVD in February 2007, *The Prestige* became the third most-rented title in the USA.

The film was directed by Christopher Nolan, a British director who has spent most of his career in Hollywood. His biggest box office success is *Batman Begins*, but for many people his most interesting film is the thriller, *Memento*.

The Prestige was scripted by Christopher Nolan and his brother Jonathan, who had written *Memento*. It had a cast of major film stars, with the main roles being taken by Hugh Jackman, Christian Bale, Michael Caine, Scarlett Johansson, Andy Serkis and David Bowie. It was nominated for two Oscars.

It is therefore already a successful film by any standards, but it also has real cinematic qualities and many original features. It seems destined in the long term to survive, a film that will entertain audiences for years to come, but it is also one that repays serious scrutiny.

It was based on one of my own books. I wrote the

novel of *The Prestige* during the early years of the 1990s, and it was first published in 1995.

Every writer must dream of having one of his or her books made into a movie, even those writers who won't admit to such a vulgar commercial desire. I was no different. I have been an established writer since the end of the 1960s. The thought of one of my novels being made into a Hollywood movie was one that always seemed unlikely and remote from reality because of the type of books I write, but the thought never went away.

I have been a regular filmgoer for as long as I can remember, with much of my life spent beneath that shaft of brilliant white light illuminating the screen at the far end of the auditorium. Film has always had an undeniable magic for me. However, my books are usually perceived as being on the literary end of the science fiction spectrum, perhaps a perverse career trajectory at a time when Hollywood was discovering what could be done with special effects and CGI. When I saw the first *Star Wars* film in the 1970s, I enjoyed it for what it was but I also assumed that as far as my kind of science fiction was concerned, and hoping to have a film made of it, the shades of night were drawing in.

The film industry is a big one, though. Many

different kinds of people make films, tastes vary, the important people in Hollywood change, and so do estimates of what will do well in the box office. In the end, the film of *The Prestige* was made and now it exists forever in the film pantheon.

From the beginning of pre-production to the film's release twelve months later I received hundreds, perhaps thousands of emails and other messages from well-wishing friends and strangers, all of them curious about one aspect or another of the film, the way it was being adapted or made, my participation in it, what I thought of the choice of actors, how different the film might be from the book, what I thought of the final result and so on. These friendly enquiries have continued, albeit at a slightly lower level, ever since the film was released. I have always tried to answer them because I realize they are enthusiastically asked, the same kind of enthusiasm I feel about other movies. People want to know about these things for exactly the same reasons as I want or wanted to know about these things.

The film is now out in the world, making its way, earning a reputation, but increasingly distant from me. *The Prestige* has in this sense become a public property, a tiny part of our collective cultural identity. However, much of it will always remain mine.

This is the story of how a single thought became

first an idea, then a book, eventually a film, finally a piece of cinema.

2. The Thought

The novel of *The Prestige* seemed for a long time to be an ill-starred book. It was not a happy book to write, although it began well.

One evening I saw a magician performing his act on television, and he finished his show with an illusion that involved making a young woman disappear in a particularly sudden and startling way. He seated her on a plain wooden chair in the centre of a bare platform, then covered her with a large sheet of lightweight material. It was possible to see her shape still there, beneath the sheet, moving her head and hands, speaking to the magician, and so on. Suddenly he snatched the sheet away, and she was gone.

Like most people who saw it, I suppose, I was impressed and flummoxed by what I had seen, or what I thought I had seen. I would probably have thought no more about it but for the fact that a second illusionist happened to be on TV the following evening, on another channel. It was the Christmas period, a time for sitting around in front of the television.

I watched the second magician without much attention until, to my surprise, I realized he was setting up an illusion almost identical to the one I had seen the day before. A chair, a bare platform, a large sheet. The only innovation was that after he had snatched the sheet away, the young woman appeared unexpectedly in a different part of the studio, smiling and waving, mysteriously transported across space. I watched the whole thing closely, but no matter how carefully or intently I looked at the screen I couldn't see how it was done.

As soon as the shops re-opened after Christmas I went to a large bookstore in the centre of London and purchased four books on magic. I scoured them for an explanation of the trick I had seen, but there was nothing there. I was beginning to grasp a fact that a few years later, when I was writing the novel, I was to learn for certain: most of the books on magic that are available to the public give few secrets away.

From these books I realized the truth: every illusion is constructed on simple principles. There are in fact six of these principles and I list them in the novel, through the journal of one of my characters. They have never changed: the great Egyptian, Hindu and Chinese magicians of the past performed their illusions with exactly the same methods. Styles change, of course, and ideas are endlessly worked on, improved, made to look more complicated or baffling.

The magician's way of presenting his tricks will also change, and novelties that enter common use will be quickly appropriated and made to work in a magical way. A trick performed in the present day with (for example) a mobile phone would not of course have been possible a quarter of a century ago, but the underlying principle would be the same.[2]

Once I began to understand the way magicians build their illusions it did not take me long to work out the answer to how the girl was made to disappear, but even before I reached it I was losing interest.

Although my reaction probably seems like obsessive behaviour, in fact I was not at that time especially interested in magic. My curiosity was aroused, but not much more. As a writer, I'm mentally open to the surprise response, something that suddenly grabs my attention, any whim, or a passing fancy. I always follow these impulses, never knowing where they might lead. Many of them lead nowhere, and for a long time it seemed that this brief interest in magic was going to be another blind alley.

However, while I was searching through the books I came across the story of Ching Ling Foo, a Chinese magician who performed in the West at the end of the 19th century. He did something with magic which *was* obsessive-compulsive, and it dominated his life, on and off stage. That interested me, and I kept the information about Ching stored mentally away.

In 1991, about 15 years after I had watched the two magicians on TV, I felt the time had come to see if I could make a novel out of these thoughts.

I knew magicians were secretive, and I knew they were endlessly curious about each other. I realized many of them were control freaks, and that they displayed signs of obsessive-compulsive behaviour. Most magicians channelled this worrying psychology into a desire to entertain and amaze an audience, but just suppose, I wondered, if two of them were to take everything much more seriously ...?

3. The Writing

I began writing *The Prestige* (it was always going to be called that, from the start) with a scene in which one of the magicians, Alfred Borden, was sitting down to write his memoirs. He worked at a desk, leaning over his notebook in a pool of light from a desk lamp. I visualized the rest of his household keeping a distance from him, being quiet, recognizing his need to be left alone. He had reached the moment in his life when he had decided to reveal all, or almost all, of his secrets.

That was all I had as an opening image, the first step on what was to become a long journey. Borden began telling his story with most of what I myself knew about magic, which was the anecdote about Ching Ling Foo. He claimed to have met Ching, and used the anecdote to illustrate the total dedication to the art of magic that illusionists need.

It was clear from Borden's admiration that he tried to emulate Ching. He stated he too had an obsessive secret, one he had kept all his life. The first draft of the novel grew from that tiny seed.[3]

The draft went slowly. I encountered many difficulties with telling the story, notably because of the complexity of the plot but also with the details of magic. *The Prestige* was the first novel I had written which required extensive practical research. Knowing nothing about magic, I had to learn everything.

I bought many different books on the subject and interviewed two magicians in person. The magic books I eventually found most useful were the ones most difficult to track down, and concomitantly expensive to buy. Many books on magic are published privately, intended not for curious members of the public or novelists writing a book, but for fellow magicians. These books are often stunningly expensive and on occasion are even protected by complicated ciphers or other security measures. One famous example, Will Goldston's book *Exclusive Magical Secrets* (which first appeared in the 1930s), was originally published with the front and back covers locked together with a padlock.[4]

Explanatory texts are highly sought after within the world of magic. Many professional magicians try to have their secrets destroyed after their deaths, or they make arrangements for their memoirs to be published for only a select few, or placed in a properly monitored secure museum or library. Some, though, do like to leave behind a written revelation of their trademark secrets.

Such explanatory texts appear as a sub-plot in my novel and were later adapted for use by the film-makers. In the film, it turns out that both magicians have kept diaries, and at different times both magicians get hold of and read each other's journal, seeking the answers which they are sure will be found within. Borden's diary, as Angier reads it, turns out to be written in code, which he soon deciphers.

Writing the novel twelve years earlier, I created Borden's memoirs in a different sort of code. It was not intended to be one of those annoying ciphers that hold you up while reading, but more as a minor puzzle which should add to the intrigue. Eventually, when the book came out, many readers managed to decipher all this, as intended. *The Prestige* was never meant to be a book of secrets.

Angier's attempts towards the end of the film to purchase Borden's secrets are commonplace amongst members of the magic community. Some wealthy magicians create archives or even museums of this sort of material – private libraries and collections of cabinets, tables, trick weapons, and so on. Like the written texts, these archives are all but impossible for researchers or members of the public to find and consult.

Another problem with writing the book was that from the outset I wanted to write a realistic novel about a subject many people find whimsical.

In the years since *The Prestige* was first published, it has been given several labels in an attempt to describe its 'type'. The publishing world is obsessed with labelling books, presumably so they can be placed on the appropriate shelves in libraries and bookstores. Although that's clearly sensible, it's a practical convenience for readers, booksellers and librarians, not a creative stimulus for writers ... or certainly not for all writers. Throughout my career as a writer I've struggled against being pigeonholed because although it's obvious that a clearly labelled book can guide readers to the kind of book they most enjoy reading, for the author who wants to try something different it means setting up expectations in the readership and market which he cannot always satisfy.

The most common label applied to *The Prestige* is 'thriller', but as an occasional reader of thrillers I must say it doesn't feel much like one now, and I didn't think I was writing one then. It has also been called a psychological thriller, a Gothic novel, a fantasy, a literary novel, a supernatural tale, a mystery, a box of tricks, a revenge drama, science fiction and good old-fashioned horror. I suppose the truth is that it is all of these things, or has elements of them all, but also it is none of them.

All the time I was writing the book I was concentrating on the demands of the story, not thinking about how it might end up being labelled as a book. The novel has three main subjects: obsessive secrecy, insatiable curiosity and more metaphorically the nature of identity. It's a novel about stage illusions, prestidigitation, magic. Conjuring is a branch of show business. The magician entertains his audience by pretending to be a sorcerer, someone who is capable of creating magic. In fact, he is doing no such thing. His performance is judged only by how well he creates the impression of doing so.

The main characters in the novel, Alfred Borden and Rupert Angier (in the film he is called *Robert* Angier), are no different from any other illusionists. They have no occult powers and they are not in contact with the supernatural. In this sense both the novel and the film are firmly rooted in the rational world. However, it was always crucial to the story that one of the magicians would try to over-reach. To enable him to do this I recruited the help of the real-life inventor, Nikola Tesla.

Tesla was something of an enigma in his day and even now not everything is known about him. His most famous invention was polyphase electricity, alternating current, but during his lifetime he patented many other electrical devices and processes, some of which are to the present day shrouded in mystery because they have never been built or at least made publicly known.

I have never understood physics, and even a day consulting the invaluable library at London's Imperial College didn't help much. While I was there, though, I did come across Tesla's diary of the time he was in Colorado, which became indispensable later in the draft.

To popularize the idea of electricity, Tesla mounted public displays or performances in which he would show how light-bulbs and fluorescent tubes would work, he made needles on dials wobble excitingly, and he got his generators and coils to emit dangerous (or dangerous-seeming) flashes and bangs.

For these reasons Tesla was thought of by many people as a showman and performer. It seemed to me not at all unlikely that magicians in pursuit of stage novelties should be interested in his work. Anything that can distract or misdirect an audience would be welcome to an illusionist. This new science of electricity, with its terrifying noises and explosions of light, would seem perfect to an innovative magician seeking an unusual form of presentation. That one of them, Alfred Borden, should go one stage further and deliberately encourage his rival Angier to think that Tesla had perfected as-yet unknown techniques, which might actually work for real, is plausible in these terms.[5]

A real concern I had during the first draft of the novel was one of credibility. I worried endlessly about the triviality of the idea. 'Who's going to care about this?' I fretted to myself, almost every day. The book seemed, somehow, not serious enough. I always take my novels seriously, and this saga of two control-freak magicians felt as if nothing in it mattered.

At one point I tried to change tack: I pitched the story at a lighter level, thinking that I might perhaps make it into a comedy, or a black comedy. But as soon as I tried that the deeply Gothic elements kept looming up: the dark family secrets, the prodigal son, the mystery in the crypt, the mansion full of deep silence on the edge of the moors. I loved all that, but the novel remained both serious and not-serious.

While the first draft was in progress I never resolved this problem. In fact, the longer the writing went on the more I doubted the wisdom of the whole enterprise. I kept breaking off from the novel in despair and writing other things. I wondered many times if I should abandon it, or even, if I did manage to complete it, have it published under a pseudonym.

I have rarely felt so lacking in confidence about a work in progress. These doubts coincided with a period of serious shortage of cash and I felt demoralized and defeated. In the end I did abandon the first draft and left it unfinished. I put the thing aside for several weeks, and tried not to think about it.

Only the need for money drove me back to it. I had written a draft of some 100,000 words. It was incomplete, only half thought out in places, and had an unresolved and complex plot that contained so many false bottoms and feints and trapdoors that I could barely follow it. However, it was most of a novel. I have to earn my living, so I had another go at it.

I write second drafts. When writing fiction I never use computer shortcuts (cut-and-paste, etc.). I print out a hard copy of the existing draft, put it on the desk beside the keyboard, and rewrite the whole thing from beginning to end. I never simply transfer material intact from the first draft, even the 'good bits' – I always re-compose everything, even if it means sometimes typing word-for-word.

So the second draft of *The Prestige* was in effect a new endeavour. From the outset I tackled what I saw as the main problem: the question of seriousness, or the lack of it.

To me, seriousness in a novel does not mean a po-faced lack of humour, or a concentration on morbid or depressing subjects. It means that the book must have some kind of relevance to the real world, that it should matter, or feel as if it matters, to the reader. Within that remit, the actual style or narration or content can then take the form most suitable to the subject. Comedies can therefore be serious, as can adventures, parodies, horror stories, satires, allegories.

With the second draft of *The Prestige*, I suddenly realized that if this feud between magicians had really taken place, then it might never have been satisfactorily resolved and its consequences would still be felt in the present day. I wrote an introductory passage set in the present, in which two of the magicians' descendants meet and try to work out what had happened a hundred years before. Goldston's book provided a template for the sort of magician's memoirs Borden might have written.

Once I had done this the magicians' own stories (Borden's memoirs and Angier's diary, the two first-person accounts which make up most of the novel and which in first draft were mostly complete) leapt into life for me. The feud was pointless and damaging, but it had a context and there were consequences. The two men should perhaps never have squabbled at all, but the disagreement was real and it affected other people. Suddenly, *The Prestige* had become a serious novel to me.

I felt the rise of certainty of purpose and the challenge that goes with it, the inner drive of writing something when it is going well. I moved along with it for several months, endlessly polishing and improving on that horrible first draft. On the way, I put in more material from the present day, describing the dilemma of the two families since the deaths of the two antagonists, and in particular the private mystery that one of the modern-day characters has carried with him throughout his life. All these were resolved in the final section.[6]

I also write third drafts. With a hard copy of the now complete second draft beside me, I rewrote the whole novel from beginning to end.

A few weeks later it was finished. It was January 1995, and the book was at last in the form in which it was published.

I was enthralled by *The Prestige* at this point. It was the first novel I had written which I felt was complete unto itself: it was coherent, serious and different, there was genuine conflict between two flawed but not unattractive characters, it had a plot that would defy anyone to anticipate, and the whole thing was a kind of meta-metaphor for itself. Usually when I complete a novel my main feeling is one of relief at having reached the end, but with *The Prestige* I felt at last that I had written a novel I was content with.

The next day I took a train to London, went to the publisher's office near Marble Arch, left the manuscript on the unmanned reception desk, then went straight home. I think it was one of the more anticlimactic days of my life, but it marked a necessary break, the start of a period of rest.

4. The Book

The passage from manuscript to book happened smoothly and rapidly over the course of the next few months. Hardcover copies were out in time for the world science fiction convention in Glasgow in August that year. The publisher paid my expenses to fly up there and sign copies.

The book was blessed with a beautiful and mysterious photo-montage by Holly Warburton, a cover image that consisted of a dove's wing and a hand, set against a royal blue background.

Unfortunately, the inside of the book was less attractive. The binding was weak, so that if handled carelessly the book would develop a curved spinal gradient. It was printed on paper that was insufficiently opaque, so that in many places there was show-through. Someone in the editorial department had changed the layout of my text breaks without my agreement, and this annoyed me. However, the book was out and the overall impression was of a handsome edition.[7]

Reviews of the novel were in general positive. Anthony Quinn, writing in the *Sunday Times*, described it as a 'magnificently eerie novel. Few recent novels have felt so vividly, indeed hysterically, imagined.' John Clute, in *Interzone*, waxed encouragingly positive: 'As an exercise in narrative control, in pretending to propound illusionary matters while never actually, I think, telling an actual untruth, *The Prestige* is exemplary. It is a lesson to us in the joy of story.'

The only really negative critique came from the novelist John Fowles, in *The Spectator*. An encomium from him about one of my earlier novels was printed on the front of the book, so perhaps he started off on the wrong foot. He could swallow neither the idea of Tesla's spectacular experiments, nor that of the bilocation they might produce. He grumbled finally that he was 'insufficiently gulled' by the book. His displeasure was a disappointment to me as I have always admired Fowles's own novels, and I considered that in some minor respects *The Prestige* was something of a tribute to him. Well, we move on.

The following year *The Prestige* won two book awards: The James Tait Black Memorial Prize for Fiction, and the World Fantasy Award.

Both of these were of course immensely cheering,

but they also puzzled me slightly. The James Tait Black is normally awarded to literary novels, and no one, not even people who had enjoyed *The Prestige*, would think of it as a traditional literary novel. And as for the World Fantasy Award ... there isn't a word of fantasy anywhere in the book. Just the Tesla stuff, and that would be only arguably fantastic. I for one would argue against it.

The Prestige was published in 1996 in the USA. My books have never been particularly well reviewed in the USA, but *The Prestige* did OK. *Washington Post*, for instance, compared the book with the works of Barbara Vine and Robertson Davies, which seemed good to me. *Publishers Weekly* made the same comparison with Davies, and in an interesting echo of what Anthony Quinn had written a year before, said the book was 'enthrallingly odd.'

Well, as reviews and awards are of only secondary importance to writers, we move on again.

A year after the first appearances in hardcovers, paperbacks of the novel were published in Britain and the US, and gradually, one by one, translations into other languages began appearing.

5. The Enquiries

Movie interest in *The Prestige* came quickly, which was something of a surprise. Anyone who publishes more than one or two novels eventually discovers that film and TV people often express interest in new books, and on rare occasions even buy an option. The amounts paid for an option are usually small or token. The rule is that such an option runs for a year or two, then expires. But with *The Prestige* two companies, one in Britain and the other in the USA, showed real interest, asked for multiple copies of the beautiful and valuable first edition – but then silence fell.

In the UK, the so-called production company wrote some kind of treatment of the book (which I was never shown, and therefore never agreed to), and touted it around the various TV and film companies in London, succeeding in having it rejected by them all. They finally gave up. They had neither paid nor even offered me a penny for the right to do this, a distinctly grey area of unauthorized use of copyright work. However, while it was going on my agent of the time and I sat quietly in the background, thinking that they might yet unexpectedly come up with something, but neither of us was surprised when they threw in the towel. I was pleased.

Once we had the book back in our undisputed control the agent started submitting it himself. One by one, all the film and production companies in London sent it back. 'But we have already rejected this project once,' they said in unison. 'We don't want to see it again.'

What they had 'already rejected' was, of course, someone else's unauthorized and unpaid-for treatment, but it amounted to the same. I had never thought of *The Prestige* as a 'project' – to me it was still just my most recent novel, but this reaction was my first inkling that *The Prestige* was turning into a package of ideas or images that other people could make something of.

Something similar to the London experience happened in the USA. A producer at Fox 2000 said he was knocked out by the book, and was determined to get it into production. This sounded much more likely.

Dazzling budgets were mentioned – film stars' names were even attached to the project. Kenneth Branagh was pencilled in to play Borden, Tom Cruise to play Angier. 'This sounds good,' I said to the agent. 'How much money are they offering?' No answer to that, it seemed, although our enquiries about the offer went regularly across to California. Meanwhile, the book, the 'project', was being shown around, apparently to everyone in Hollywood. I started to feel nervous, because by this time I had found out what happened when it became a project in London.

The Fox 2000 interest ended suddenly. The producer was fired, and that was that. As his ship sailed slowly into the sunset, he yelled back to the shore that his commitment to *The Prestige* was as firm as ever, but soon he had vanished forever over the horizon. Later we found out that one of the main reasons he had been canned was his irrational attachment to a project called ... *The Prestige*. The powers that be at Fox 2000 clearly did not want to make a film about Victorian magicians.

Time went on passing, as it does. During the next couple of years I changed literary agents, though not for any of the reasons perhaps hinted at here. Circumstances change. I moved to a large agency in London, one which maintained its own TV/film department, and which had links to other agencies throughout the world.

As a result I acquired in the USA a real Hollywood agent, one who specialized in selling books for adaptation into film. Her name was Dabney Lee, and when she read *The Prestige* she sent an interesting letter to my London agents.

'Although *The Prestige* doesn't fit the obvious Hollywood movie mold,' she wrote, 'I believe that it's a fantastic story with incredible thematic cogency that features uniquely complex and charismatic characters.' She added that she had already recommended it for consideration to a number of executives around town. This sounded promising. Also promising was the change in London – my new TV/film agents began resubmitting *The Prestige* with great energy.

I soon discovered what the product of such activity meant.

All over the film world, talent scouts, script consultants and production assistants started asking to see copies of the book. Many of them worked for impressively famous names. The first time I saw a copy of a letter written from an office on Sunset Boulevard, and headlined with the name of a prominent director or producer, I thought my luck had changed forever. I soon learned that these enquiries were routine trawling expeditions and carried no more likelihood of an eventual sale than an enquiry from someone I'd never heard of, but as the weeks went by, each such enquiry gave my pulse a pumping flurry of anticipation for a few seconds.

My agents were only too happy to order extra books from the publishers, and day after day, week after week, dozens of copies of the novel went whizzing optimistically in the direction of anyone who had asked for one. Whether the book was read and considered by everyone who asked for a copy is anyone's guess, but I know for certain that I never heard another word from about 99% of these people.

I did, though, get the bill for their copies. Every time the agents had any money to send me, their accounts department enclosed a copy of the latest invoice from the publishers, and they deducted the cost of the books. Sometimes this bill ran well into hundreds of pounds, and I don't like to think what the total came to over the period of a year. It was a drain on my income I could little afford. I tried to be optimistic, thinking that in the end something must come of it all.

In the end, something did.

6. The Offers

It was the beginning of the year 2000, five years since I had delivered the novel.

Following many hints, rumours and quiet conversations, the agents finally reported that they had now secured three positive interests. These were real. They were all from producers who were keen to convert their interests into firm offers, and as soon as possible after that into contracts. In increasing order of attractiveness, the offers were as follows:

The director Julian Jarrold, working with the British television channel FilmFour, wanted to make a one-off TV film. Theatrical release might or might not be involved. Although the money on this was not very good, I was none the less interested. I had met Julian Jarrold and seen his work on TV. I thought he was skilled and individualistic. I had also met Adrian Hough, the writer with whom Jarrold wanted to work – again, Hough had an impressive c.v. Another attractive feature of this offer was that Jarrold said he was ready to start straight away, and would treat *The Prestige* as his next project.

The second offer was from a theatrical producer in New York, working with the director Sam Mendes. Mendes had just made *American Beauty*, a film I had already seen twice and admired a great deal. The money being offered was good and the overall quality of the people behind the offer was impressive.

But then there was an offer from a small production company called Newmarket Films. They were working with a director I had never heard of, Christopher Nolan. Their cash offer was slightly better than the Mendes one, but all offers come with extras and provisos attached, so it isn't always the lump sum payment that on its own is the most important. For this reason I felt the two offers were on more or less equal footing in financial terms.

I was sorely tempted by the Mendes offer. *American Beauty* had been sharply directed, the photography was brilliant and the script was literate and subtle. The film had already won Golden Globes and BAFTAs, and was soon to sweep through the Oscars. At the time I received the offer, *American Beauty* had been nominated for eight Academy Awards, and a couple of weeks later it won five of them (including Best Picture, Best Director and Best Script). Whichever way I looked at it the Mendes offer was of the highest quality. I ached to accept it.

Word of this must have reached Newmarket, because I was quickly sent a bundle of enthusiastic reviews of Nolan's first film, *Following*, as well as a VHS copy of the film itself. Attached to the cassette was a Post-It Note. It said: 'Have a look at this film, then try to imagine what the director might do with the technical facilities of a major studio behind him.'

That struck me as an intelligent approach, so I watched *Following* immediately.

It is a short (70 mins) film in black and white, using borrowed equipment and unknown actors. Christopher Nolan himself operated the camera. Although many notches above the level of an amateur film, *Following* clearly showed the problems of a low (or non-existent) budget. Judged ruthlessly, you could see it had not been made by someone with the technical facilities of a major studio.

I sensed a kindred creative spirit in Nolan. He seemed to think about things in the same way I did, he attacked a narrative with the same disregard for sequence, he obviously had the same interests in reality, perception and unreliability. He was clearly talented, but what interested me was that his talent was quirky, unusual.

Perhaps with hindsight none of this seems surprising, because of what Nolan and Newmarket have achieved since. On that day in 2000, though, nothing was obvious. Newmarket had made or distributed only a few films, none of which had made much of an impression. Ahead lay singular Newmarket films like *Donnie Darko*, *Whale Rider*, *Monster* and *The Passion of the Christ*, but they were ahead. Christopher Nolan himself was a beginner, young and unknown, and it would be a considerable act of faith to favour his offer.

Logic told me to grab the Mendes offer and count my lucky stars, but once I had watched *Following* there was really no contest. I had a hunch that Nolan was the better bet.

I backed my hunch and told the agents to accept the Newmarket offer. Fortunately they agreed, and said they were convinced that in the long run it would turn out to be the right decision.

7. The Contract

The first part of the 'long run' soon became apparent. It takes weeks and months to draw up and agree a film contract, and the weeks and months dragged slowly by. Most of the year 2000 went past without any apparent progress. I knew by this time that Nolan had already completed his first studio film, *Memento*, although I knew nothing about it. I assumed he would make *The Prestige* next, but clearly nothing would happen until we had agreed the deal.

Memento opened in the UK in November of that year. I went to see it on its opening evening at the Curzon Picture Palace in Bexhill. I was naturally curious about it and had no idea what to expect.

The first thing you see in *Memento* is the word 'Newmarket', confident white letters on a black background. Who takes notice of or remembers the producers' identification logo cards before a film begins? I never had in the past, but I did that night. *Newmarket*. They were real, they really made films!

('Where's that contract you've owed me for months?' I thought grimly in their general direction, as the card faded away. The weeks and months were taking their toll on my patience.)

The first 80 seconds of *Memento* are now famous, but that evening I went to see it was long before anyone took notice of it.

The first image in the film is a close-up of a hand holding a Polaroid photograph. There is something round and blue in one corner of the picture – the rest shows blood spattered over a white tiled area. The credits are shown briefly over this image, while moody music (by David Julyan) creates an unmistakable sense of dread. The hand shakes the picture a couple of times, in the way people do while the Polaroid image is forming. But this time when the hand steadies again, the image is starting to fade. As we continue to watch and the credits end the picture fades away to invisibility. Time is moving in the wrong direction.

The hand inserts the Polaroid paper into the base of the camera, the motor drive paradoxically sucks it inside, and the actor Guy Pearce takes a photograph. *Flash!* Large droplets of blood are seen running up a wall. We see an empty shell case on the floor, a pair of blood-spattered spectacles. We see the back view of a head lying on the ground, presumably someone dead or wounded and apparently the owner of the spectacles. A gun flies up into Guy Pearce's hand, and he kneels down and points it at something. The shell case rolls across the tiled floor. The spectacles fly into the air. The head moves. The shell case enters the gun. The gun goes off. The man lifts his bloodied head from the floor and shouts something incoherent, perhaps: '*What?*'

The film begins. I realized my fists were clenched with tension and the hairs on my arms were standing on end.

This short opening sequence has subsequently become a classic scene, one that is discussed in university media studies departments and taught in film schools. It is an undoubtedly brilliant sequence, not just in the way it has been shot and edited, but in the way it creates a visual metaphor for the whole of the film.

As is widely known now, *Memento* is about a man suffering from short-term amnesia: he can't remember more than about the last twenty minutes at any point. What he needs to remember he draws on a wall chart or scribbles into a scruffy dossier, or even writes or has tattooed on his body. He takes Polaroids of what he thinks he will need to remember, and scribbles identifying notes on the bottom of them.

The story is told in a series of short scenes, each of which depicts events which took place before the scene you have just been watching. This reverse narrative device is at first confusing to the audience, but you quickly get the idea. It has an extraordinary effect: the audience too is made to suffer short-term amnesia.

Our expectations of narrative have been developed by thousands of novels, films and TV drama. We are accustomed to the convention of chronology, where one narrative step logically follows another, so that we take into each new scene the memory of the last. *Memento* brilliantly throws that away: we can remember nothing as the story proceeds.

One scene, for example, opens with Guy Pearce sitting on the lid of a toilet in a motel room. He is holding an empty bottle of whisky. He is looking dishevelled and unshaven, with a scratch on his face. 'I don't feel drunk,' he says, mystified as to how he got there. He sniffs his armpit, then goes through and takes a shower. His mystification is the same as ours. It is only when the next scene is shown, and then only at the *end* of it, that we discover how and why he ended up on that toilet seat, in that motel room. But by then more mysteries have appeared and once again we are trying to fill the holes in our memory.

The film goes on to its conclusion. Pearce is driving through the streets of suburban Los Angeles, still knowing nothing about what he has done, or what he is about to do (although this is the end of the film it is also the beginning of the story). Suddenly he brakes to a halt outside a tattoo parlour. The first of his memories is about to be inscribed on his limbs.

'Now, where was I?' he says. The screen goes black.

I walked out of the cinema feeling stunned. *Memento* was clearly a completely original piece of work. It had come to Britain more or less unheralded. Although decent money had been spent producing the film it had not arrived in a cloud of publicity (or if it had, the publicity had passed me by). Not particularly liking violent thrillers, I probably would have given the film a miss if I hadn't known Nolan was behind it.

The film came as a shock to me but not because of its violent scenes. For all its gruesome subject-matter – Leonard, the character played by Guy Pearce, is motivated by the earlier murder of his wife, and moves through the demimonde of drug-dealers and petty racketeers in search of the culprit – *Memento* was subtle, witty, innovative, brilliantly photographed, acted to perfection, and raised many intriguing questions about memory, identity, truth and the nature of reality.

I drove home from the cinema, convinced that in choosing the Nolan offer I had made one of the best decisions of my life.

The next morning the contract from Newmarket

arrived in the mail. It seemed a propitious moment.

I spent most of that day reading and trying to understand the contract, speaking to the agents about the dozens of clauses, mostly written in (to me) impenetrable American legalese. The advice I was given was that although the contract terms were modest on the scale of things in Hollywood, it was a good-enough deal for a first film sale. The agency reminded me of my novice status, of Nolan's youth and obscurity, of the fact that Newmarket was a small, independent company.

I signed.

One quirk of the contract that was new to me: the American lawyers required the contract to be notarized. It seemed to me to be an unnecessary flourish, but one that had to be obeyed. I traced the only Notary Public in Hastings, made an appointment for the end of the afternoon, and took the bulky document down to his office for the near-ceremonial procedure.

That evening I went back to Curzon Picture Palace and watched *Memento* a second time. Ray Sutton, who owned and ran the cinema, spotted me walking in and was obviously curious about why I was there for the second night running. I couldn't resist: I blurted out my news.

'You couldn't talk the distributors into having their British premiere in Bexhill, could you?' Ray said when I had told him the story.

I would agree to anything that day. As I left at the end of the evening I tried to imagine the crowds of fans in Bexhill's humble Western Road, the red carpet stretching for at least six feet across the road, the stars' limos fighting for parking spaces on the seafront ...

8. The Insomnia

It transpired that *The Prestige* was not after all destined to be Nolan's next film. Shortly after we agreed the contract I read somewhere that he had taken on the Hollywood remake of a Norwegian thriller called *Insomnia*. I had already seen this when it was released in 1997, and because I knew the film I found the choice puzzling.

Written and directed by Erik Skjoldbjærg, and starring Stellan Skarsgård, *Insomnia* had two unusual qualities. The first was that it was Norwegian, the second was that the whole story took place in the endless daylight of a summer north of the Arctic Circle. Watching the film had an insidiously unpleasant, disjunctive effect. The collapse of the central character's diurnal rhythms soon started affecting the audience too. I remember yawning my way through the second half, shifting uncomfortably in my seat, wishing the film would end.

I wondered what Nolan would do with the story

when remaking it. Presumably he would not film it in Norwegian, but I supposed the weird effect of the endless daylight would give the film the same nerve-racking edge as the original.

When the leading actors were announced I began to understand more of the appeal the project must have held for him. With Al Pacino, Robin Williams and Hilary Swank in the main parts, Nolan would be working with three recent Oscar winners. Shot on location in Alaska and Canada, and with a budget of some $46 million, *Insomnia* would obviously confirm his position as a leading Hollywood director.

I slowly realized that the excitement of the bidding for my book at the beginning of the year was not going to be matched by a rush into production, so I allowed thoughts of *The Prestige* to fade into the background, where they were less distracting. During this period I was in the thick of finishing my novel *The Separation*, and had little time to think of anything else.

9. The Announcement

The months and years began to slip by once again. Newmarket faithfully renewed the option when the time came, but it was difficult to gain any hard news from them or anyone else about when *The Prestige* might start production, if ever.

In the spring of 2003 there was a flurry of excitement, and it arose from a reliable source: *Variety*, the Hollywood trade paper. There it was, on the front page of the issue of April 16, 2003:

Nolan wants 'Prestige'
'Memento' director to work on magic movie
By MICHAEL FLEMING

The story said that Christopher Nolan's next film would tackle the world of magicians with his adaptation of *The Prestige*. Disney and Warner Bros would be sharing distribution rights. The script was complete, a budget had been prepared and everything was ready to go. Jude Law's name was being connected with the project.

This sounded pretty good to me, but at the end of the article an ominous doubt was raised.

Nolan, the article said, was expected next to direct 'Batman,' resurrecting the Warner franchise with screenwriter David Goyer. The script was already in progress. However, the article concluded, because the development time of a super-hero epic was always a long process it was still possible that *The Prestige* could step in front of it.

The point about the development time of a super-hero film was a crumb of comfort, which for a while I clung to. Only I, not *Variety*, knew the eagerness with which Nolan and his company had sought the rights to my book. I still trusted in that. Maybe I was being naïve. I was warned by friends about Hollywood hype, the easy promises and flattery and the single-minded obsession with pulling off fast deals, but so far I had found the Newmarket people straightforward and reliable. I accepted what they said when they told me, through my agent, that they were still excited about *The Prestige* and expected Chris Nolan to film it as his next project.

Only three months later, though, in July of that year, *Variety* announced 'Batman' as a definite Nolan production, with a release date in 2005. Could this be really true? It seemed so: when I enquired, Newmarket told the agent that Warner Bros were holding an option on Nolan and wanted him for the next Batman film. *The Prestige* would follow immediately after, they said.

Once again I believed the information from Newmarket, and although I knew I was in for a further long wait I returned to my real life. It would take at least two years for 'Batman' to be developed, started, filmed, completed and released, so I put it as far to the back of my mind as possible.

At this stage, the Batman film to be directed by Christopher Nolan did not have a proper title, although internet sources were guessing at variations and permutations of Batman-type titles. The film was of course eventually released as *Batman Begins*.

It was around this time that I discovered Google 'Alerts', and began to use them.

Google allows you to set up a series of recurrent searches for any word, or words, or string of words, and whenever their vast database encounters them it alerts you with an email message containing a link to the internet site or page where the mention occurs.

I therefore entered 'Alerts' for Christopher Nolan and Emma Thomas (the Newmarket producer who had been in contact with me, and who is, in fact, Nolan's wife), and another, with a slight but unmistakable feeling of egotism, for my own name. I also put in the word 'prestige' as a search string.

The following day Google sent me the first half-dozen of what would turn out to be, in the years ahead, many thousands of such website addresses. It became a daily chore to work through them, hoping to pick up clues about what might really be going on with Nolan and *Batman Begins*, but more interestingly to me what the rumours and predictions were about *The Prestige*.

10. The Alerts

For the next two years, Google Alerts were my main source of information about what was happening. No one else gave me any news at all.

At first the pickings were discouragingly thin. Although I would receive about ten or twenty notifications every day, almost none of them told me anything I wanted to hear.

For instance, most of the alerts from the word 'prestige' turned out to refer to the aftermath of the shipping disaster off the coast of Spain, when an oil tanker of that name had caused widespread marine pollution. I also learned a lot about 'the prestige' of certain governments – this was something usually spoken about by minor officials working for dodgy dictatorships. There was a cervical implant called a 'Prestige', a table-tennis bat called a 'Prestige', a record label called 'Prestige', a brand of chocolates called 'Prestige', a cooker hob called 'Prestige', a funeral director in Scotland called 'Prestige Burials' ...

and many more.

'Emma Thomas' was apparently a successful British hockey player.

There was an Irish autobiographer called 'Christopher Nolan', and my Google entry for 'Chris Nolan' produced a steady stream of entries about a prolific blogger, as well as an American journalist, a football coach and a police chief in Fairbanks, Alaska, all with the same name.

I also discovered there was a footballer called 'Christopher Priest', but even more surprisingly a top British close-up magician called 'Chris Priest' (you realize there must be people out there in the wider world with the same name as your own, but I didn't expect to come across a magician), and of course my own long-term doppelgänger, the American comics writer James Owsley. A few years before, Owsley had irritatingly changed his name to mine, causing professional confusion that continues to this day.

It was ironical to realize how many namesakes and doubles we all appeared to have – particularly in view of the subject-matter of *The Prestige*, and several other of my books – but it was taking me nowhere.

The conclusion I drew from all this was that the real Christopher Nolan did not seek publicity, got on with his job without releasing much to the press or public, and probably did not spend much time on the internet. The only website dedicated to him was an unofficial one run in a lacklustre way from Germany. There was something rather solidly reassuring about this, since the internet normally seems wide open to anyone who wants to blow their own trumpet. But at the same time it was a little frustrating for me because I felt I had a legitimate interest in trying to keep abreast of what was going on.

What was actually going on, of course, was that he was working on his new film, *Batman Begins*.

It wasn't long before it sunk in that almost every Google hit on the 'real' Christopher Nolan took me to a comics-related website.

The news that the Batman franchise was being revived with a new film was causing a palpable stir in those circles. Most of the excitement seemed puerile and idiotic to me – the speculation was usually along the lines of which villain Batman would have to fight, and which actor would play the Penguin, or Two-Face, or one of the other Batman characters – but I have never been a fan of comic-book super-heroes, so it is no surprise this sort of thing left me cold.

Anyway, I could hardly be expected to feel enthusiastic about the production, as it was sitting squarely in front of any prospects for mine. I accept my view on this is a non-typical one.

There was something else too.

What had attracted me to Nolan's work and made me accept his offer was what I had perceived to be a singular talent – a rare imagination coupled with an unconventional way of telling a story and some genuine cinematic skill. The clues to this were there in *Following*, and abundantly revealed in *Memento*. Since then, Nolan had directed a remake of a pedestrian Norwegian thriller (admittedly a superior remake), and now he was spending two years on a Hollywood block-buster based on a risible comic character. It seemed an inexplicable waste of his time. I was disappointed by this, and felt disillusioned with him.

Google kept sending me over-excited internet comments from comics fans, where they were obsessed with the belief that Nolan was going 'revive the franchise.' What this meant was that he had announced he was going to imbue some realism or back-story or plausibility to the Batman motif. As if that mattered!

Anyway it missed the point. You can't make a silk purse out of a sow's ear. Batman is shallow because all comics from that period are shallow. That's part of the idea. American comics present simplistic issues in black-and-white, sketch them out in uncomplicated lumps and moralize vacuously about them. Problems are not real ones but are motivated by plot twists, and are resolved with violence or fantastic acts of heroism.

In other words, graft on as much psychological

realism as you like to the thin material of a comic-book hero, film it moodily, add subtle music, spend a fortune on elaborate sets, but you will still end up with a body-builder in a bat-mask who jumps off buildings.

Of course, I believed I understood why Nolan would want to make such a film. It would firmly cement his position as a top Hollywood director, and therefore, the argument presumably went, *Batman Begins* would put him in a better position to make a more intellectually challenging and less commercial film like *The Prestige*.

All this was irrelevant to me, in my singular position. I knew that *The Prestige* was material ideally suited to the early Nolan, and in its own way was highly commercial, or certainly had real commercial possibilities. It made me impatient to think about this. I didn't want to sit on the sidelines forever while Christopher Nolan's directorial career went from one daft blockbuster to the next.

None of this had been helped by the release in 2002 of Sam Mendes's next film after *American Beauty*. *Road to Perdition* was also based on a comic-book story, although not a super-hero one. It starred Tom Hanks, Paul Newman and Jude Law, and was a classy, good-looking and well acted production. It wasn't to my mind nearly as subtle or as well written as Mendes's earlier film, but at least it was there, up on the screen, finished.

I couldn't help thinking wistfully, as I sat in the local cinema, that had I made a different choice from the offers I received, I might instead have been watching *The Prestige*, up there on the screen, finished.

11. The Batman

In the summer of 2004, Newmarket's option on *The Prestige* expired again. They promptly renewed it for another 18 months and said to the agent, encouragingly, that they didn't need any more time than that as Christopher Nolan was on schedule to start work on it as soon as *Batman Begins* had been completed. This was more or less exactly what I wanted to hear, and a calm feeling of confidence crept over me.

However, the general internet blackout of news continued and within a few weeks I was feeling jittery again. A new and worrying ingredient was being added to the mix.

The release of *Road to Perdition* had been one thing, but that was already in the past and anyway was about the choices I might or might not have made about the original offers. The existence of that film did not in itself have a bearing on *The Prestige*. But at the beginning of 2005 I began to notice something that might.

Rumours were appearing on the internet about a film in development that was about Victorian stage magic. At first, I assumed these were educated guesses about *The Prestige*, or that the production company was releasing 'teasers' about it.

Neither of these was true. In April 2005, a new film went into production in Prague, called *The Illusionist*. It did not take me long to find out more about it. Written and directed by Neil Burger, it was to star Edward Norton, Jessica Beale, Paul Giamatti and Rufus Sewell. It was an adaptation of a short story by Steven Millhauser, a writer I admire who is much less well known than he deserves. With more than a few feelings of alarm I dug out my copy of Millhauser's collection *The Barnum Museum*, and re-read his story.

My first feeling was relief. Millhauser is a unique writer and in some ways the story 'Eisenheim the Illusionist' is typical of his work, without being the best he's done. The story was much as I remembered it: it was a relief to be reminded that it was nothing at all like *The Prestige*, not least because the rationale of the story is a supernatural one. The movie would not of course necessarily follow the story, so the risk remained that other people might think there was overlap, but I was confident that the plot of my novel was unique. However, 'Eisenheim the Illusionist' certainly had the same sense of theatricality, the same period setting, it had an illusionist as the central character, it included the performance of baffling magic. These elements are all present in both works, but they are only on the surface. To many people, superficial similarities between films can often seem deeper than the real subjects, something that was to become rather painfully clear later.

I assumed that if I had come across news of this film then Newmarket and Nolan, on the spot in Los Angeles, must certainly know about it.

If they were concerned about it they did not act on the concern, because in the end *The Prestige* of course went ahead, but for several weeks I was anxious about the possible negative effect of *The Illusionist* on *The Prestige*.

Clearly, it was coincidental that two independent directors should each make a film about illusionists. At the same time it seemed likely to me that neither production knew about the other until things were so advanced there was nothing that could be done.

The Illusionist was due to be completed at least a year before *The Prestige*, but I knew, of course, that Nolan's film was not a copycat of Burger's, nor was Burger's film an attempt to 'spoil' Nolan's. It was just one of those things, no matter how it might appear to others.[8]

Batman Begins opened in Britain in mid-June 2005, about a year into Newmarket's renewed option for my book. I went to see it on the first day.

It was a skilful and professional film, but it just wasn't my kind of thing. I thought it was overlong, simplistic and dull, in spite of the constant noise on the soundtrack, the huge sets and the fast-moving events. The many fight sequences looked unconvincing to me, with the use of much soundtrack grunting and banging to cover up the surprisingly inept action.

The special effects were of course clever, but these days they are something audiences tend to take for granted – in any event, Warner Bros had spent $150 millions making the film, so one can realistically and justifiably expect the result to look good. But, lamentably, the much advertised sequences which suggested a psychological background were underwritten and trite. The mood changes in the film went from scenes which were fast and noisy to scenes which were slow and less noisy.

Intriguingly, it appeared that a large proportion of the rest of the audience agreed with me about the dullness. They were mostly of the age-group whom one would assume were the ideal target audience for such a film (while I am neither ideal nor typical, as far as audiences for Batman movies go).

About halfway through the film I reflected that if I

had been involved with making it I would have felt depressed and discouraged by the behaviour of the audience. Many of them talked throughout the film; a lot of them changed seats, seeming more interested in spotting their mates than following the story; several of them went disruptively in and out of the auditorium, to get drinks, or to visit the toilet. They seemed less than completely gripped by the film.

On the other hand they had turned out in large numbers, because the cinema was packed. Perhaps that's all that matters with a super-hero film. Speaking for myself, I was glad my only connection with it was incidental.

The DVD of *Batman Begins* was released four months later. I bought a copy, not because I wanted to see the film again but because I was interested in the extras always found on DVDs. In particular, I wanted to gain a glimpse of Christopher Nolan at work, hear from some of the crew and actors who had been working with him, and above all listen to what he had to say about the film. I also hoped he might have something to say about his future plans.

Frankly, I found his comments about the film as uninspiring as I had found the film itself.

Nolan spoke in a lively way, but had little to say that gave much away. He explained how they had written the script (in his office at the back of his house!), how Christian Bale had put on weight and gone into training for the role (too little weight, then too much, then he got it right!), how the other members of the cast had been chosen (they're all wonderful actors!), how the sets had been built (they were huge!), how they had designed the Batman costume (it had to be body-hugging and frightening and black!).

Of his commitment to the subject of the film, Nolan said that he had talked the Warner executives into giving him the directing job by telling them that he would take the super-hero story and 'treat it in a realistic fashion.'

He also said that Bruce Wayne's background had never been dealt with in any of the earlier films, so he tackled that. Nolan described how Wayne was traumatized by bats as a child, then witnessed his parents' violent death, became conscience-stricken by his own immense wealth and the appalling levels of crime in the city – and that's about it. The simplistic content of comics-sourced material was never set out more plainly, if inadvertently.

According to the material on the DVD, the only part of the film-making process that seemed genuinely to excite Nolan was the fact that the studio had commissioned the building of a 'real' Batmobile – that is, one that could be driven. This went really fast, and was terrific to play around with!

Nolan either had little of any interest to say in his interview about the making of *Batman Begins*, or if he did he chose not to say it. The unmistakable impression I gained from watching the DVD was that he secretly realized that *Batman Begins* was not, in fact, much of a challenge to him. Naturally, he was not going to bite the Warner hand that fed him.

Batman Begins had clearly presented him with several demands on his skill, notably those of scale, expense, time, technical difficulties, but those will arise in any big production. Other than that, it wasn't a story that had stretched him.

Memento must have stretched him – so too would *The Prestige* if he did it properly. His Batman epic was obviously hard and probably enjoyable work, and it took care and expertise, the resources of a major studio and the contribution of hundreds of others. But for all the noise and the millions of CGI bats and big sets and explosions and cars going fast and men in bat suits jumping off buildings, it obviously hadn't made him think.

Nolan in fact seemed half embarrassed that it took a film like *Batman Begins* to position him as an A-list director in Hollywood.[9]

However, that is what the film did, and that is what he had become. By the time I saw *Batman Begins*, Nolan's position in Hollywood was secure.

Furthermore, and for me the only thing that actually mattered, he had at last begun pre-production on *The Prestige*. The years of uncertainty were suddenly at an end. In the last week of September 2005, I was invited to dinner in London with Aaron Ryder, the producer of the film, when he told me in no uncertain terms that the green light for *The Prestige* was on, and that pre-production would be starting the following week.

12. The Expectations

The news from Mr Ryder did not come as a complete surprise, because various hints had been reaching me for some time. When I started receiving emails from assistants in his office, making an appointment to meet him in London, I guessed he wasn't going to fly all the way from California to tell me that he and Nolan had lost interest in *The Prestige* and were going to film something else instead. However, it was good to have everything confirmed, and from the horse's mouth. A faint feeling of unreality began to settle about me, one which has never really dispersed since.

Until this meeting, the project called *The Prestige* had seemed to me a private one, something that was coherent because it was on a small scale. It involved no larger group than me, my agents, the producers and the screenwriters. But almost immediately after this meeting it enlarged into something much bigger and more difficult to envisage, and therefore it felt to me more unmanageable.

The Hollywood process was starting. Vast sums of money were being talked about, famous film stars were being chosen for the acting roles, prizewinning technicians were being employed to build the sets, design the costumes, create the photography. Names of personalities and studios that had been familiar for many years, but in a distant sort of way, became the background to my daily life: Michael Caine, Warner Bros, David Bowie, Disney, Scarlett Johansson, amongst many others.

And in this process of transformation from a small project into a huge production, I became increasingly irrelevant to whatever was happening.

In some respects I didn't mind at all. I had my own work to do and my own life to lead. Film-making is not my world. I had nothing to contribute to the process, so I didn't feel too put out by being put out. I believed my book was in good hands, and I was content to leave things as they were.

When I signed the Newmarket contract for the deal, I didn't expect much. I did expect the agreed sum of money to be paid up front if the film was made, and in the meantime I expected options to be taken out regularly and promptly to keep the deal alive if the film could not be made immediately. In these matters, Newmarket were exemplary. They tended to leave decisions about renewing the options until the last possible minute, but they never delayed, were never late. Money was paid correctly and in full on the day it was due.

Other than that, my expectations were low.

If the production went ahead I didn't expect to be consulted about the size of the budget, or who the most suitable actors might be, or where the film should be shot, or who the technical crew should be, or for that matter about any of the thousands of decisions that have to be made when setting up a big production. In the event, they did go ahead and unsurprisingly I wasn't consulted on any of them.

Nor did I even expect to be consulted about the book, the adaptation of the book, or the writing of the script. I wasn't.

In fact, I was happy not to be consulted. Once I had seen *Memento* I realized that the Nolan brothers knew what they were doing, and the best thing I could do would be to lie low and let them get on with what they were good at. The adaptation they made and the script they wrote is entirely their work, and I had no part in it.

However, the script is the direct link between the book and the film so no one should be surprised that I take an intense interest in it.

13. The Screenplay

Although I was never formally consulted about the script, Newmarket sent me an early draft. It was dated March 2003, and carried a single by-line for J. Nolan (Jonathan). Christopher Nolan at this time was still busy filming *Batman Begins*, but he apparently worked on later drafts and polishes of *The Prestige*.

I had re-read the novel of *The Prestige* not long before they sent me this version of the screenplay. The novel was due to be republished in paperback by Gollancz, and in the normal course of production they sent me the proofs for checking. Obviously, I knew by this time that the Nolans' adaptation was in preparation, so while I was going through the book I had tried to look at it with fresh eyes, imagining how I would adapt it to a screenplay were I given the job. I had no idea what the Nolans had in mind for it, so I was able to look at the novel in an open-minded way.

I learned what many before me have also learned: that the writer of the original novel is not the best person to adapt it to the screen.

Frankly, I couldn't see the wood for the trees – it was impossible for me to decide which parts of the novel should be left out, or changed, or combined, or enhanced. *The Prestige* is a tightly plotted novel, and although it's a long book every page contributes directly or indirectly to the complicated story.

I fully accepted that it could not be filmed from the page, but even so I could not see where it should move away from the page. I wanted to leave everything *in* (or at least could think of half a dozen good reasons for doing so), when I knew should have been trying to find ways of taking stuff *out*. It was difficult for me to see how.

A few weeks later, Jonathan Nolan's draft screenplay arrived. Reading it was revealing and also instructive.

He ruthlessly chopped the order of the story about, combined scenes and characters, he changed wordy sequences into visual ones, and in several places he conveyed complicated ideas with skill and economy.

The opening pages, with the voice-over about the *Pledge*, the *Turn* and the *Prestige*, made a particularly strong impression on me. Nolan had taken a few hints from the novel, had presumably done some research of his own into the ways of magicians, had had a think about everything, and finally came up with this simple, memorable and powerful narrative hook. I was witnessing the writer of *Memento* hard at work, and he had done an expert job. I was impressed.

I had a few reservations about some parts of the screenplay as it then existed. One or two of the dialogue scenes had characters talking about ideas that had already been established visually, but I could imagine that these would be smoothly removed by a later rewrite. It seemed to me that for a few pages in the middle the story lost its drive and direction, but again I knew that what I was reading was not the final version.

Then there was what Nolan had done with the ending.

The ending of the novel is a complex one. A large number of shocking or at least startling ideas are condensed into a short sequence, deliberately underplayed, with several loose ends left for the imagination of the reader to consider. The novel ends swiftly on an ambiguous note, but if the reader has followed the plot to this point, he or she should be in no doubt about what is going on and what the ending means.

I wrote the final scenes in that way as a calculated risk. While always wanting to tie up a book neatly, I know that the novels that have made the deepest impression on me as a reader have been the ones that left me wanting more. If you write an ambiguous ending you lose the definiteness given to a story by a final resolution, and some readers don't like that. On the plus side you gain memorability.

When I was writing the novel of *The Prestige* I knew exactly what had happened at the end of the story, but to lay it out in literal terms ran the risk of seeming banal. Resolving an intricate mystery in definite terms will raise in many readers' minds the unwanted question: *Is that all?*

I therefore opted to leave most of it unsaid. The mystery of the missing twin might or might not be solved, the identity of the man hidden in the crypt might or might not be clear, the story might or might not have reached a firm ending, but at least something has happened, clearly and shockingly.

Over the years I have read and heard many different reactions to the ending of the novel – some people have been hostile to it, but many more people have enjoyed the shiver of horror that my gothic excesses provided. As far as I can tell, everyone I have heard from, favourably or otherwise, has understood the ending. Almost everyone remembers it.

What the Nolans would do creatively with the ending of the film was something that I had been quietly speculating about over the years.

It is self-evident that what works on the page doesn't necessarily work on the screen. The problem for Nolan would be that to use my ending from the book would have meant taking on board many complex and time-consuming plot strands, and they would probably have weakened the main part of the film.

The conclusion of the novel, like the beginning, is set in the here-and-now. It always seemed possible to me that one way of adapting the book would be to move the whole story back to the 19th century, when many of the main events took place. This would place it clearly in a recognizable social context, one that had the objectifying effect of distance from our own world, but also one that had comprehensible links with our own world. However, to remove the story from the present day would mean that the ending in the novel would no longer be possible.

It was a dilemma. I couldn't see how it might be done, and I was glad it was someone else's problem. If anyone could come up with a solution, I thought, it would be the Nolans.

So, while I read the draft screenplay, I looked forward with curiosity and professional interest to what they had done with the ending. As the screenplay unfolded it was not easy to see where their story was heading. For me, it had so many haunting similarities with the novel that I was frequently confused by it: had I written that scene, or was it something devised by Jonathan Nolan, or was it an adapted version of my original?

There were obvious differences all the way but just as many subtle similarities, so it was difficult to read it 'cold'. The best way to read a script under normal circumstances is to try to visualize each scene, and create a mini cinema screen in your mind, so you can at least guess at what the scriptwriter was thinking. With the screenplay of *The Prestige* I was constantly distracted by my memories of the novel, what I intended, what the impact should be.

As the climax approached I realized what Jonathan Nolan had done. The secret of Alfred Borden was being kept back until the end, the very end. In a welter of explanations, cut-aways and flashbacks, Borden made his revelation to Angier. Then he himself learnt the shocking news about Angier's own deception. The truth about both men was at last out. There was a reprise of the opening words, the brilliant narrative hook spoken by Cutter, and the story ended.

I found it both satisfying and worrying. It was satisfying because it was so clearly a professional job, executed with real skill, tremendous imagination and a willingness to depart from my original while staying within the general ambit of the novel. I read the screenplay two or three times, trying to learn from it.[10]

Although the screenplay's conclusion was neatly done and was cohesive within its own terms, it was also worrying.

The structure of the film story was built around the ending: a concealment from the film's audience, a surprise kept out of sight for as long as possible. It seemed to be a large risk to take, especially as so much of the commercial market for a film is based on word-of-mouth recommendations. If people were going to recommend *The Prestige* to their friends, what could stop them revealing or at least hinting at the twist ending?

It reminded me of the twist ending in *Psycho*, and the lengths to which Alfred Hitchcock had to go to try to keep people from revealing his secret. (Forty years later, when Hitchcock's 'secret' is known to everyone, prior knowledge of the ending does not detract at all from the quality of the film as a whole.)

And there was the matter of *definiteness*. The Nolans' screenplay of *The Prestige* ended with what amounted to a deathbed confession between the two main characters. All was laid bare, explained, shown.

When I was reading the script again I looked more closely at the way this was set up in the adaptation, and in fact it is brilliantly done.

I realized that the Nolans were structuring the story

on the classic Hollywood three-act model – there are many how-to books about writing screenplays, dedicated to this rule. However, that classic format had been subverted subtly into the three 'acts' claimed for standard stage illusions: the *Pledge*, the *Turn*, the *Prestige*.

The effect was clearly intended to structure the plot as if it were an illusion. It seemed to me that they didn't quite pull it off, simply because the various reversals and revelations in the story endlessly brought in complex and multi-layered diversions. But the Nolans had none the less made an heroic attempt at it, and I could see how they were doing it. Meanwhile, other magical methods were being deployed in the script, in particular misdirection and sleight-of-hand. It was an audacious idea, a brilliant conceit, and further underlines my belief that this is a masterpiece of a screenplay, but it was still a tremendous risk to conceal the secret about Borden.

A screenplay, cold on its pages, is one thing: a film decked out in wide-screen colour, with music, effects, costumes, actors, is quite another. I knew I was reading an interim draft, and that rewrites and further revisions were inevitable. The script I had been sent was merely an insight into what they had been thinking, rather than the final effort.

Anyway, no one was asking me for an opinion.

They had sent me a copy of the screenplay only because I had requested it – no one was seeking my collaboration or suggestions. It seemed to me that as a film-maker Christopher Nolan knew exactly what he was doing. I thought it best simply to wait and see what he did with it.

14. The Secrecy

From the day pre-production began I heard almost nothing more from the producers. Because my expectations were low, I hardly noticed the blanket of silence and certainly didn't worry about it. I assumed someone would contact me if anything came up that involved me, but in the meantime I carried on as normal. Somewhere on the other side of the world they were preparing to make a $40 million film out of my book, but you wouldn't have known it from the difference it made to our daily lives.

The new year began and with it, punctiliously paid, came the purchase price for the film rights. This was due to be paid on the first day of principal photography, but because the option was about to expire Newmarket paid it a week or two ahead of time. I knew from that moment that the film was certain to be made. In fact, photography began in Los Angeles on January 23rd 2006, a date I elicited from chance remarks on the internet. Google's Alerts were still bringing in my daily crop of gossip, but were now my primary source of information.

Life carried on as before, but at last something was changing. Word had spread beyond my family and immediate circle of friends, and I started receiving many interested enquiries about the film, mostly by email but also whenever I met anyone who knew something about what was happening.

'How's the film going?' was the constant question, always friendly, encouraging, supportive.

To which my constant answer, the invariable but true answer, was, 'Sorry, but I don't know.'

It was these repeated enquiries that did make me wonder about what in fact *was* going on. I gradually realized that although I didn't mind in the least about not being consulted, the feeling of not knowing anything at all was annoying.

Writers with similar experiences in the past told me until I was tired of hearing it that in Hollywood the scriptwriter was at the end of the 'food chain'. But even he or she was not at the absolute end. That lowly position was reserved for the author of the original book.

It certainly seemed to be not only true but habitual, so not to be taken personally. None of this really bothered me: I've been a freelance writer for forty years, and the life of a writer is not what it might sometimes seem from outside. I don't see it's worth complaining about, and never did.

It shouldn't have surprised me, but the filming of *The Prestige* seemed to provoke a new rush of internet gossip about the much anticipated (but then imaginary) sequel to *Batman Begins*.

Every morning I would skim through the Alerts that Google sent me, only to find one comics website after another excitedly reporting rumours or making guesses about who would star in the next Batman film, what the story would be, who the villains would be played by, even what the possible title could be, and other fan stuff. Some of these people even assumed that *The Prestige* was in fact a code name for a Batman sequel. Nolan's name and reputation had become so closely tangled up with Batman that a considerable section of the public naturally assumed that from now on anything he did would be Batman related.

In mid-February, barely three weeks after production of *The Prestige* had begun, I read a report that Jonathan Nolan had written the screenplay for the next Batman film and it was already in pre-production. That was clearly nonsense, but it gave some idea of how obsessively interested some people were in this so far non-existent film, and how eager they were to see it made. Into the bargain, it was clear that the reality of

The Prestige, the Christopher Nolan film that was actually in progress, was less interesting than the wished-for one he might make next.

There was perhaps a salutary warning in this for Mr Nolan.

One day I noticed that *The Prestige* had gained a page for itself in IMDb, the Internet Movie Database. There was no information there about the film that I did not already know, but I saw that a discussion forum had started. There were already several threads running, so I joined up and began reading.

I found myself witnessing an apparently endless frenzy of fan speculation, nearly all of it concerned with the coincidence that both Christian Bale and Hugh Jackman had recently been cast in other films as superheroes. What seemed fascinating about *The Prestige* to these people was that the story was based on a 'feud' and therefore was likely to be, in their minds, a titanic struggle between Batman and Wolverine. The most argued-over question was about which of the two was likely to 'win.' I must say I found the banality of these arguments pretty discouraging. The 'controversy' raged for week after week, as futile a discussion as it was possible to imagine.[11]

I hung on as a silent observer, hoping that some grains of genuine information might leak through all the fan speculation. In the end, some did.

One intrigued me: it was from an actor who had been given a small part in *The Prestige*, and he described what his couple of days on the set had been like. Almost as an afterthought, he mentioned the fact that the entire cast and crew had had to sign confidentiality agreements. As he was apparently free to talk about having worked on the film (and he mentioned other actors' names), it seemed that the confidentiality surrounded not the existence of the production itself, but the story, the twists and turns of the plot.

Later, I saw another actor's blog, claiming much the same. Details of the shoot were being kept under wraps.

Another hint of this growing obsession with secrecy came in an unexpected communication from Newmarket.

People were always asking me where the film was being shot, and my standard vague reply ('Um, they're filming it in Los Angeles, I think') didn't satisfy them or me. So I looked it up and within seconds found the info on a public page in IMDb.

The astonishing information was that the film was mostly being shot in Los Angeles! The crew were filming in a theatre in downtown L.A., a large house in Koreatown, L.A., a newspaper office in downtown L.A., Mount Wilson on the outskirts of L.A. – and so on. I put this apparently harmless information on my website. Within a day or two an admonishing email came from Newmarket, saying they didn't want me to reveal the locations, as these were secret.

Chastened, I took the information down from the site immediately, but wondered if anyone at Newmarket ever looked at IMDb.

More to the point, how did the information reach IMDb in the first place?

It felt deeply ironic to me that a story inherently about the dangers of obsessive secrecy should be surrounding itself in a fog of secrecy.

Of course, I realized what was going on. The twist ending I had read in the draft screenplay, with the shock revelation laid bare, must still be in place, and it was assuming the proportions of a commercially sensitive business scheme that would be vulnerable to industrial espionage.

There are many precedents for secret endings in the film world. *Psycho* is probably the most famous, but others that came to mind immediately included *The Sixth Sense*, *Gambit*, *The Usual Suspects*, *Fight Club* and *Sleuth*. All of these films turned on a surprise revelation at the end (or, in one case, at the beginning). All of them were thought likely to be at risk of losing business at the box office if the plot gimmick was widely known before anyone saw the film.

I too have always had a dislike of reviewers 'giving away' elements of my stories which I prefer readers to discover for themselves. For writers of books this is more of an irritation than a threat to income, so I do understand why film-makers might feel more protective of their secrets. However, in most of the examples above, the films followed the original appearance after only a short period. I was often tempted to point out to Newmarket that by the time it was being filmed *The Prestige* had been on public sale in the UK and USA for more than twelve years and was available in translated editions around the world.[12]

15. The Veto

While the filming went on in the secret and unguessable location of Los Angeles, in another universe, it seemed, my foreign rights agents were quietly going about selling translation editions of the novel. One by one, more countries and languages were signed up: Polish, Portuguese, Croatian, Russian, Hungarian, Japanese, Korean ...

Of course, the original book in English was still available in Britain and the USA, as it had been continuously since 1995 in both hardcover and paperback editions. With the coming of the film, though, the English-language publishers were keen to bring out new tie-in editions in paperback, to try to capitalize on the publicity created by it.

In particular, my American publishers, Tor, were anxious to obtain 'key art' from the distributors to use on the covers. Key art is based on the poster for the film, or publicity photographs taken during the shoot, and naturally becomes associated in the public mind with the film itself. Although it is expensive to buy, and can be awkward to arrange (if the actors' likenesses appear in the photograph or artwork then their permission too has to be obtained), the boost in sales justifies the expense and trouble.

Unexpectedly, Tor found themselves stonewalled. Neither the production company, the studio nor the distributors returned their calls.

I was not too concerned at first. I assumed, and I think the publishers also initially assumed, that while filming was going on small details like production stills or publicity photographs would be low in the film-makers' priorities. But the weeks went by with no progress, and publishing deadlines started to loom.

Although the novel had been on sale for so long, with steady success, it had not been a best-seller in the sense most people understand the term, and I was rather looking forward to the idea of there being a tie-in to the film. Times have changed from the days when the rubric *'Now a major film'* on the cover of a book would guarantee blockbuster sales, but a surge in sales does inevitably follow. I saw the existence of a film edition of my novel as a bonus, a direct way in which I could benefit financially from the film. I also felt justified in believing that *The Prestige* was a 'real' novel, seriously intended, one which had already made its way without the help of a film. I thought if people enjoyed seeing the film they might like finding the novel too.[13]

With *The Prestige* already in existence as a completed novel the publishers at least had the luxury of not having to commission the writing of a special book. As a matter of fact, both British and American publishers had recently reissued the novel in the ordinary way about a year before the film was expected to be released, so the text was conveniently in place. All that needed to be arranged or settled was the cover for a new edition, and what would appear on it.

In July 2006 (with the film already scheduled for release in the USA three months later, in October), I received an urgent email from my American editor: Tor had exhausted all possible contacts and lines of approach, and unless in the next two or three days they received a firm commitment by the distributors to their use of the key art they would have to abandon their plans of producing a tie-in edition. They asked if there was any way I could intervene to solve the problem.

On the day I received this I was staying in a lakeside five-star hotel in Switzerland, a guest of the Neuchâtel International Fantasy Film Festival, for which I was on the jury. My only internet access was through an expensive hotel broadband line. What could I do to influence anyone? Rarely have I felt so removed from the centre of things. Tor and I sent a few depressed emails to and fro – asking *'have you tried this?'* and so on – but it was clear they had come to the end of the road.

No one involved with filming *The Prestige* took it seriously as a book, or at least that was how it seemed to me. Perhaps it had outlived its perceived usefulness when the film was made, because in their terms the film might seem to have improved on the novel, or in effect replaced it.

I could partly understand that. The film production was an immense enterprise, a project which had been in preparation for several years. It employed hundreds of people, the company had spent millions of dollars. It had taken three months to be filmed, and it was currently in the lengthy process of post-production. The original novel, now in the production company's terms improved upon, now 'replaced', probably no longer seemed all that important to anyone except me and the book publishers.

But people who read novels and people who go to films are often the same, and there is a definite pleasure for many people (myself included) in either going to see a film based on a novel with which you are familiar, or reading a novel from which a film you've just seen has been adapted. People like to know that there's a book behind a film. You can gain insights, one from the other, a fruitful cross-hatching of ideas and impressions and images.

And there's a practical commercial justification too. Publishers put copies on sale, together with appropriate publicity material, in places where films are rarely if ever publicized. When did you last see a film advertised in an airport, a shopping mall, a supermarket, or, of course, a bookstore? With a prominently displayed paperback, looking like the film, informing or reminding people that the film has come out, both the film-makers and the original writer of the book can reap valuable rewards.

It seemed the film people weren't interested, though.

After I returned from Switzerland, this discouraging matter dragged on without resolution. At one stage Tor editor Jim Frenkel actually spoke to somebody at US distributors Disney, but was asked why it was so essential for the publisher to have the book on sale 'before' the film appeared. The Disney spokesperson grumbled that the director didn't want the ending given away by the book. (Did Nolan think that no one had read the book in the twelve years in which had been continuously on sale?)

In the end, at the last minute, Tor lashed up a home-made cover for their paperback, an all-typography effort. '*Fall 2006 – A Major Motion Picture*' it said bravely on the cover, but that wasn't the point. It didn't look like a tie-in to the movie, simply because it didn't look anything like the movie.

In Britain, the publishers Gollancz managed to obtain the rights to the poster for their edition. This pleased me and surprised me because I assumed that the key art was never going to be made available anywhere in the world. Since then, the key art has been used on translations and other editions around the world. Some publishers even rejected it, preferring their own artwork.

So why were the American publishers blocked in this way?

The comment from Disney about the director not wanting the ending given away was just hearsay, but in time Christopher Nolan's own concerns did become known. He gave many interviews to promote the film. These cropped up regularly in the week before the American release of the film in October, and his concurrence with what Disney had said to the publishers was clear.

Asked repeatedly about the relationship of the film to the original novel, Nolan said in essence two different things. His choice of words obviously varied from one interview to the next, but the contradiction of what he was saying didn't change.

In the first place, he said that he and Jonathan had

made a free or loose adaptation of the novel, and everything in the film was substantially different from the novel.

For example, in an interview with Sheila Roberts for the website *moviesonline.ca*, he said:

> '*It's a loose adaptation but one that hopefully is true to the spirit of the novel. The novel, if you've read it, is a big sprawling book with a lot of different possibilities for a film but one that certainly can't all fit into a screenplay. So it took us a long time to focus on the elements we thought that would really work.*'

In several other interviews Nolan repeatedly explained that the ending in the novel would no longer fit in the film, because it was set in the present day and he and Jonathan had made the decision to avoid that strand of the story.

In other words: Nolan was saying that the film was different from the novel.

But the second thing he said was a warning against the book. When the film opened in Britain, he gave an interview to *Empire* magazine, which was typical. The interviewer mentioned that he had already read the novel.

'"*You shouldn't read it before you see the film*," Nolan said, groaning. "*It spoils everything!*"'

In other words: Nolan was saying that the film was

not different from the book after all.

It seemed to me Nolan was clearly trying to have his cake and eat it. When he thought about the film he had made, the story had become different from the novel (improved upon, replaced). When he thought about the novel I had written, my story was something that now existed mainly to spoil the enjoyment of his film.

Nor did Nolan mention that the screenplay had just been published in book form: Faber & Faber brought it out in both the USA and the UK on October 31st 2006, a week before the film opened in London. There could be no prevarication about this. If you read the Nolan's published screenplay before you saw the film the ending would be incontrovertibly spoiled. But that was Nolan's book, not mine. It's horses for courses.

16. The Preview

Thirty years ago I was a reviewer for a monthly magazine called *Film,* published by the British Film Institute, and aimed at the numerous film societies that operated under the aegis of the BFI at that time. Once a week I would go to a press show in London and see two or three films in a small viewing theatre somewhere in the back streets of Soho. There were never more than about a dozen other reviewers there. We assembled in a loose group, watched the film in half-light, scribbled our notes and headed off in different directions at the end. That was what I understood to be a press show.

The Prestige received its London press show at the end of October in a large, multi-screen cinema in Leicester Square called the Vue. I turned up on the evening in question and was at once struck by the size of the crowd of people surging around in the lobby. Upstairs, the bar was also packed. I assumed by the sheer number of people there that they were paying customers for one of the other films. Innocently, I wondered what it could be that would attract so many people. The reality of the size of the launch of *The Prestige* slowly dawned on me.

Everyone seemed to be in a cheerful mood, anticipating the film. After waiting around for a while I went into the auditorium, found a good central seat in the stalls and settled down to wait. Slowly, the place filled up. In fact the auditorium filled up completely, the last arrivals having to search around for the few remaining empty seats. It was a huge cinema and it was full. The finding of the last seats took so long that the start of the film was delayed – a cause for mundane anxiety, as my last train home was due to leave not long after the scheduled end of the viewing.

At last Jayne Trotman, a representative from Warner Bros (the European distributors), appeared in front of the stage and made a brief introduction to the film. She added some words that were printed on the first page of the press kit, which I had been handed on the way in:

'*The Prestige* is a mystery structured as a cinematic magic trick. In order to allow audiences to fully enjoy the unfolding of the story, the film-makers respectfully ask that you not reveal too much about the deceptions at the heart of the film.'

This is tactfully phrased and unobjectionable (and

in the event, almost everyone who reviewed the film honoured the request), but for me it was further confirmation that the film depended on its central secret and was trading on the quality of surprise.

The lights went down. There was a preview of another upcoming Warner film, then *The Prestige* began.

Apart from a few glimpses from the trailer of *The Prestige*, which had been viewable on the internet for several weeks, I had no idea what was to come.

It is in fact an extraordinary experience to see something you've written adapted into another format. And not half-heartedly adapted: Nolan's film of *The Prestige* is a full-blooded professional movie, directed, performed and mounted with marvellous style and expertise. It is a considerable film, well thought out, beautiful to look at, told in a complex and intelligent manner, and making repeated demands on the audience to concentrate, to listen, to follow the complicated story and to relish the subtleties.

On one level of my mind I was aware of all that, but I was also endlessly fascinated and distracted by the similarities to and the differences between my book and the film. I had gone there telling myself that whatever changes had been made would not matter, and that was still essentially the case. What I hadn't anticipated was how *interested* I would be.

First one scene, then another, was slightly different from the novel, slightly the same. There were several exchanges of dialogue that used different words to say something I had expressed. I had been prepared for this by reading the early draft of the script, but even so I found the adaptation distracting. I wanted to take in the film in the same way as everyone else on the first viewing, simply enjoy the story, but I was constantly aware of differences.

For example, Angier's wife Julia, a character from the novel, was killed off in the first few minutes of the film. (In the novel, Julia is a significant character who survives to the end.) But then Borden's wife Sarah, who is barely in the novel at all, featured in scene after scene. Nor was it just a change of roles. This was new material, introduced by the Nolans for reasons I understood but which were no longer true to the heart of the novel – Julia's influence on Angier was reduced to providing a motive for Angier to revenge her untimely death; Sarah's influence on Borden grew into a touching sub-plot about marital love. Their roles in the novel are different in many ways.

Early on in the film there was a flashback to Angier's visit to Colorado, which only occurs towards the end of the novel. Then there was a flash *forward*. Had I done it that way? While I was trying to remember how I had written it, another scene had begun. I recognized the characters, but not the situation. That had been changed, but it still worked in a familiar way.

For me, the experience was rather like the one I had had with *Memento*: I kept being distracted by matters I had forgotten, and matters I thought I should remember.

For these reasons it was difficult on this first viewing to be objective in any way about the film. It grew easier after the first hour. I began to relax as I grew used to the incomparable experience, and by the end I was thoroughly enjoying myself.

However, time was flying. My unarguably last train home was a few unremarkable minutes away from departure at Charing Cross Station. I waited to see my name flash up on the credits, then ran for the exit. Out in the cool autumnal evening the world seemed unchanged, but I was renewed within.

17. The Release

I was to see the movie of *The Prestige* twice more before its relatively short period on cinema screens came to an end. I felt it was a film to relish on the big screen while I still had the chance. Like the majority of people these days I watch many movies at home on DVDs, but the silver screen still has an undoubted extra edge.

At all three theatrical showings the audience was apparently wrapped up in the story. No one fidgeted, waved to their mates, answered their text messages, went out for a popcorn refill. The cinema audiences were silent, seemingly absorbed by the intelligently told but complex story.

The Prestige is a film without the usual ingredients. With one short exception it lacks scenes of fast action, which are almost *de rigeur* in modern Hollywood movies. There are hardly any jokes or amusing situations. There are no love scenes, no sex scenes. No car chases, no gun battles. No songs or dancing.

Almost no spectacular scenery. Most of the action takes place indoors, lit with an amber hue, while the characters debate or argue or explain or try to deceive. There are scenes set in theatres before live audiences, and these are lavishly done, but ultimately they too are included to form part of the debate that is at the heart of the story.

It is an entertainment film, but it is also a film of words, of arguments, of conflict or inner questioning. It is driven by plot and ideas, not by character. It works at a sustained and skilful level of approachable cleverness, drawing an interested listener into the disputes that arise between the two proud, misguided illusionists.

Audiences do not normally have their minds stimulated by big-budget films, and I was intrigued by the response I witnessed in the audiences. As I left after all three of the screenings, I heard people arguing about the film, discussing it, all the way down to the street.

From the middle of October 2006 the reviews of the film were coming in thick and fast, notably from the USA. Google Alerts duly sent me long lists of them every day, and at first I conscientiously read them all.

As a published novelist of some four decades' experience, I have grown used to the way in which books are reviewed. For one thing book reviews appear intermittently – one or two are usually printed in the first week the book is out, but the rest straggle in over the next two or three months. The compensation for this is that most reviewers appear to have read the book properly, and in their reviews they come up with their own ideas about it.

Reviewing of films, I discovered, is almost exactly the opposite. In the week a film is released there is saturation coverage, which is more noticeable in the USA simply because a film opens in many different cities on the same day. Seeing so many reviews at once I quickly realized that press coverage of movies, at least in the USA, is endlessly formulaic and repetitive.

Most of the reviews I read of *The Prestige* appeared to be quickly written journalistic pieces from whoever the newspaper's regular film critic happened to be, drawing heavily on the material in the press kit, and usually accompanied by one of the four or five stills released to the press by the distributors. Except in one or two exceptional cases original observations about the film, or insights into it, were all but non-existent. Opinion and taste were well to the fore.

The standard format seemed to be: a brief plot synopsis ('two nineteenth century magicians get into a deadly feud'), some background information (usually about Nolan's previous films, but often also about the stars, particularly Bale, Johansson and Bowie), comments about the film's content, then at last a brief evaluation, pro or con. Most seemed pro, incidentally.

Perhaps such a summary does not seem all that unremarkable, but when you read one piece after another you soon realize that it is a form of journalistic shorthand, with remarkably little interest in the actual film. To read such articles one after the other is a frankly boring experience.

Almost none of what appeared was original. For instance, the film opens with the memorable narrative spoken by Michael Caine that I have already mentioned admiringly, about the *Pledge*, the *Turn*, the *Prestige*. It's good writing, and a brilliant way of opening the film. The full text is reproduced at the beginning of the press kit, and so, with stultifying predictability, it was quoted again and again in these newspaper reviews.

Presumably this kind of superficial reviewing is useful to readers who want to decide what movie to see at the weekend, but it has almost no other merit. No doubt the distributors would see an endorsement of the film as cheap advertising. Perhaps with that sort of thinking, as an interested participant you soon start mentally counting up the 'good' reviews and hope they outnumber the 'bad' reviews.

As criticism, though, such journalism is all but

worthless because it says nothing to anyone in the cast or crew, or to the producers, as a discussion of what they have done. Nor does it assess the film's worth, or try to place it in a larger context, or make relevant connections with or comparisons to competing works.

I imagine that an experienced director like Nolan would find these reviews frustrating and annoying, and I suspect he doesn't bother to look at them. I certainly lost interest in them after the first two or three dozen, and for me reading film-reviews from an insider's perspective was a new experience. For someone who has been in the business for a few years it's probably an irrelevant and depressing thing to do. I began to understand the deep cynicism many people feel about reviewers.

With the publication of the reviews, here in the UK as well as in America, it was clear that the 'private' nature of the film had emphatically come to an end. It was now at last a genuine product, Hollywood's latest, out in the world for all to see.

It was also now something that was regularly described as 'Christopher Nolan's *The Prestige*'. This change of proprietorship took a bit of getting used to, but I didn't really mind and still don't. It is incontrovertibly Nolan's film, but I have the novel to myself.

18. The Adaptation

The first image in the film is a tiny scene that runs for no more than about fourteen seconds.

Under the superimposed title of the film we discover we are in a clearing in woodland, where a number of top hats lie in a heap on the ground. The film's title fades away. The camera tracks slowly across the hats. Borden's voice is heard off-screen: '*Are you watching closely?*' The screen goes black.

There is nothing to locate this scene in context, but later in the story it will become apparent that we are in the forest that grows over the slopes of Pike's Peak, in Colorado. It is here that the Croatian-American inventor Nikola Tesla (played by David Bowie) has built a laboratory, where he is running a series of secret experiments into the nature of electricity.

The magician Robert Angier (played by Hugh Jackman) has travelled to Colorado to meet Tesla, with the intention of commissioning him to build a matter-duplicating apparatus that he can use in his stage act.

He mistakenly believes that his rival Borden is already in possession of such a device, and is using it in his own stage performances.

In my original novel, Tesla tests the device by transmitting a piece of specially marked metal through it. The Nolans deftly substituted this with a more visually arresting image: Angier's own top hat. Any physical object would work as well as any other from Tesla's point of view, but a pile of shining silk hats in a forest clearing is unusual and intriguing. There's something additionally anomalous about the hats, which in this fleeting glimpse we cannot know or suspect, and that is that the hats are all identical to each other in every way, duplicated many times. A black top hat is of course widely recognized as one of the standard tools of the magician's trade. With marvellous economy, the Nolans have established two of the main themes of the film in this brief scene, as well as the general ambience of mystery and magic.

But there is one more level. The voice we have heard is that of Alfred Borden (played by Christian Bale). Most of the audience would probably not be able to distinguish Bale's voice from any other, with these four quietly uttered words, but it is significant within the syntax of the story that it is the character Borden speaking to us.

The off-screen narrator in a film often becomes the

audience's confidant, the setter of scenes, the link between the events seen in the action and their relationship to the narrator's voice. We instinctively trust the voice-over, and even if we do not we listen attentively.

By opening with the sound of Borden's voice, the character is being made into a signature, given a form of supremacy over other characters. This would seem from the outset to be Borden's story.

But is that so? We are not informed of anything in these four brief words. The voice-over does not take us into its confidence, the owner of the voice is not identified and the scene is not set. Indeed, the contentious tone of voice is almost a challenge to the audience. Borden asks us only if we are watching closely. The implication is of course that we are *not*, which we instantly realize as soon as we hear his question and are regarding the blank screen.

Later it will emerge that Borden has been manipulating Angier: the trip to Colorado was set up by Borden as what was intended to be a wild-goose chase, a hoax, a settling of an old score. When we know this, those opening words of Borden's, apparently directed at the audience, could also seem to be said ironically to Angier. *'Are you watching closely?'*

We know nothing of this, at least on a first viewing

of the film, so we can assume, and safely, that the question is directed at us. We know we should be on our guard, or that we are being warned to be. But at the same moment as we heard the question, the mysterious image disappeared

What were we really looking at just then? What were those hats? What was it about them we were supposed to notice? And why do we need to watch them closely? Too late – they have vanished.

Already in these first fourteen seconds, the uniquely complex and subtle nature of the film has been set out. We will be shown familiar things in unfamiliar circumstances, we will be challenged by them. We will see something, assume we understand it, then be made to realize that perhaps we did not. This leitmotif runs through the whole film.

Nor is this opening shot a mere narrative hook, a gimmick. Nolan has not done with us yet. Immediately following the shot of the hats, we are propelled directly into the main story with a surprising and effective transition.

We fade in to find canaries hopping around in their cages, chirruping happily. A voice-over begins, but in a breach of narrative convention it is not the same voice. Like the one we have heard a few moments before, this voice has a London or Cockney accent, but Borden sounded argumentative, gravelly, challenging.

The new voice-over is lighter in tone, more reasonable and persuasive. We are no longer being directed to watch or notice or work things out for ourselves – this voice seems likely to explain to us what we need to know. We warm to it, wait for the information we need. As the voice-over begins, the familiar face of Michael Caine comes into view, and we assume that this has become his narrative.

Caine's voice-over is not identified by the actions we see on the screen – it sounds like an omniscient viewpoint, a diegetically internal voice addressed to no one apart from the audience. However, Sir Michael's voice is a famous one, and for the contemporary film-goer at least there is no question that the voice is his and that it belongs to the character we see him playing.

Michael Caine is in the role of Harry Cutter, a retired magician now working as an *ingénieur* – a deviser and builder of magical apparatus who is employed by a magician to work for him behind the scenes. (Later in the film he is sometimes addressed as 'John'.) He speaks the words which have become the trademark, iconic words of the film: '*Every magic trick consists of three parts, or acts ...*' Cutter is explaining the mechanics of magic to us, and he has become our confidant. In a switch that is so far unexplained, he has taken over from Borden as the focus of the film's narrative.

Cutter is, or soon becomes, the moral centre of the film, the reliable character whom we can trust and believe, and who at first acts as a mentor to both of the young magicians whose feud is the heart of the story.

As Cutter speaks, spelling out the syntactical logic of the *Pledge,* the *Turn,* the *Prestige*, the complexity of the film's storytelling is revealed to us.

Cutter appears to be performing an illusion for a small girl, who watches him with rapt attention. He selects a canary, takes it in his hand, holds it out towards the child.

Cutter's voice-over says, '*[The magician] shows you something ordinary, a deck of cards, or a bird ... or a man.*'

The scene suddenly cuts away from the small girl – now we are in a crowded theatre, where an audience is staring with the same rapt attention towards the stage. The glimpse of the people in the audience, all wearing the Victorian or Edwardian style of clothes, is the first unmistakable sign in the film that we are not in the present day. On the words '*or a man*' the camera pauses on the face of a young, bearded man.

Perhaps he is recognizable to a contemporary audience as Christian Bale, playing Borden ... but in fact (the film audience can't know this yet) Borden is *himself* in disguise, with a false beard and moustache. His left hand is concealed by a glove. Why? Even though the audience of the film cannot suspect what is going on, the layers of the film's unique complexity are already piling up. The disguise of Borden's face and hand are both crucial to the plot.

Syntactically, is the presence of Borden in this scene, at this moment, part of Cutter's argument? Cutter is saying: '*The magician shows you something ordinary ... a man*', and we have paused on Borden. Is this man, this Borden in disguise, the '*something ordinary*' that is part of an illusion?

While we are still absorbing the idea that '*a man*' might be part of the illusion, we cut to the magician on the stage. This is Angier, standing in the spotlight, raising his arms at the start of his trick. There is no introduction as to who he might be, no visual clue or identification. Is this man instead the one Cutter is talking about, who might be '*something ordinary*'? Or does that description apply to them both?

In two tiny sequences, Christopher Nolan has rolled up his sleeves, flicked his wrist and performed a stunning sleight of hand. The story's elements are unobtrusively in place, stacking up like magical apparatus waiting at the side of the stage to be trundled into the spotlight.

We think of course that we are at the beginning of the story, but in reality we are already watching events that take place close to the *end*, although there is no hint of that to an audience watching the film for the first time. Furthermore, there is no time to learn or realize any of this because the film is moving swiftly on, and Cutter's narrative is still in full flow.

He continues his description of the way a trick is performed, and the film cuts to and fro, between Angier performing his illusion at the theatre, and Cutter himself showing the small girl a trick with a canary. Both sequences proceed, acting as startling counterpoints to each other. On the one hand there is Angier's terrifying and mysterious display with the forking electrical discharge of a Tesla coil, and on the other Cutter's own small trick, making a canary seem to disappear in front of the child.

It is clear something is going wrong at the theatre. After Borden has used his disguise to gain access to the stage so that he can closely inspect Angier's magical apparatus, he is accosted by a stagehand. Borden was disguised with the intention that Angier would not recognize him, but now he has strayed off-stage. He rips away the disguise and contemptuously announces to the stagehand that he is a part of the trick. He then ducks down to the below-stage area. He is there when Angier completes the part of the illusion called the *Turn*, dropping through a trapdoor in the stage into the huge tank of water waiting below.

While Cutter declares that the third act of an

illusion is called the *Prestige*, it's clear that Angier is about to drown inside his tank. Borden watches helplessly from outside as Angier struggles frantically to escape from the water.

At this point, Nolan strikes again at our expectations. We discover the source of the voice-over.

It is not as it has so far seemed, an internal narrative from Cutter to the audience, illustrating the scenes we have been watching. It turns out to have been diegetically external all along. We discover that Cutter is in the witness box of a courtroom, and that he is giving evidence in a trial.

Borden is in the dock, clad in handcuffs, accused of Angier's murder. Everything that we have heard so far from Cutter has been an explanation to the jury of how a trick is performed.

We are only three minutes into the film, and already we have been made aware of at least *seven* levels of plotting, if not in full detail then certainly in enough outline for them to have been memorably established:

1. Tesla's experiments with a matter duplicator (so far unexplained, but well set up by the scene of the hats);

2. An element of what looks like magic in Tesla's experimental work;

3. Borden's hint that we, the audience of the film, are

not seeing everything we think we are seeing, and
that we should be on our guard, that we should
watch closely;

4. Cutter's role is as an explainer of magic, partly in
an indirect way to the audience of the film, but also
directly to the jury in a courtroom, where Borden is
on trial for murder;

5. From Cutter's explanation we learn that stage
magic is structured to convert the ordinary into the
special, or special-seeming;

6. Angier is killed when his illusion goes wrong, and
Borden has been accused of interfering with the
working of it in some way, thereby being
responsible for the murder;

7. Cutter's relationship with a child, apparently at this
point in the film a relative, or a child who is close
to him in some other innocent way.

The film's incredibly complex time-structure has
also been adumbrated in these first few moments of the
film.

The scene with the canary and the child looks like
a quiet opening, but the events take place at the end,
the very end, of the story – it is in fact the *Prestige* of
The Prestige. Because you haven't been watching
closely, and the film-maker has ensured you think you
have seen everything but have not, you can't know
that. Later, you will. A memorable reprise lies some

two hours ahead.

The revelation of the hats lying in the forest glade is from the middle of the story, the second act of the film (the *Turn*, if you like).

Cutter's voice-over, his evidence in court, is spoken several weeks *before* the scene with the child which it overlays, and several weeks *after* the sequence in the theatre, which it also overlays.

The trial itself must, of course, have taken place after the alleged murder, which we seem to be witnessing, although in fact it is not a murder at all.

The scene that follows these opening sequences occurs in Newgate Prison *after* the jury's verdict. The judge does not pronounce the guilty verdict in the film for some time to come, and the scene after that is a flash *back* to the sequence in Colorado, where Angier visits Tesla, before the hats, before the scene in the theatre, before the trial, long before the trick with the canary.

This sounds as confusing as a plot-synopsis of Joseph Heller's novel *Catch-22*, but structural complexity is not the same thing as confusion.

In the film, the quiet lucidity of the argument, the steady photography, the authoritative sense of place, the skilful storytelling, the atmospheric music, all these take the audience through the many devious layers in a smooth and assured way. You might not fully understand everything you see, but you can certainly follow it.

I do not intend to go through the entire film scene by scene, but I wanted to examine the opening because it confirms my belief that the Nolans have made a brilliant adaptation of the novel.

There is nothing in what I have described here that has been taken directly from the novel. For example, the scene in the theatre where Angier drowns is a variation on a lesser scene in the novel, a significant rather than crucial one.

In the film Borden is beneath the stage of the theatre at the time Angier falls through a trapdoor into a tank waiting below, which leads to Angier's death by drowning inside it. Borden thereby becomes implicated in Angier's death.

In the book Borden actually interferes with Angier's magical apparatus and accidentally precipitates the disaster.

No one in the film's audience could know the significance of this alteration to the plot, but it is the moment in the film where Christopher Nolan deliberately turns his back on the ending of the novel. It is an example of pure filmic adaptation. The end was changed from the beginning.

In the book, Borden's interference with Angier's

apparatus sets in train a sequence of events he can not have foreseen: it leads directly to the destruction of his own career, and to the remarkable transformation that Angier undergoes. The film leads only to a trial for murder.

The scene in the courtroom is therefore not from the novel, and although it is short and succinct it serves as a useful means of conveying a great deal of information to the audience through the short sequence of cross-examination that we observe.

Michael Caine's performance in this scene has great conviction and plausibility, and if anyone watching the film to this point was feeling bewildered after the complexity of the opening scenes, it is here that the story starts to take on what seems to be a linear form. The questions and answers, quietly put by the advocates, and replied to by Cutter in a direct and informative manner, start to fill in the background of what is going on.

Later, after the courtroom scene, Cutter visits the warehouse in which Angier's magical apparatus is being stored. He is accompanied by the judge who has been presiding over Borden's trial, and together they are inspecting the matter-duplicating device that Tesla built.

This is another sequence that has no precedent in

the novel, and follows the earlier scene of Cutter's cross-examination. (In the film a few other scenes come between the two court sequences, such is the complex narrative.) To enable Cutter to maintain his professional secrecy about the device, the judge has promised that he will allow Cutter to explain its working to him in private.

This scene is where the two men meet to discuss the Tesla device, and to my mind it is a problematical one.

For one thing, it is far from clear to the audience of the film that the man we see standing with Cutter is the judge. We last saw him in his judicial wig and gown, and a lot of plot has gone by since then. In this scene he is wearing 'civilian' clothes and a silk hat, and it is not at all obvious who he is. Only when Cutter refers to him as '*Your Honour*' do we get a reminder that he is the trial judge. (In fact, he should have addressed the judge as '*My Lord.*')

The point of the scene is for Cutter to tell the judge, and of course the audience, that the working of this apparatus was not magical, but real (i.e. the apparatus is scientifically based). The judge also enquires about a large glass tank which is in storage beside the Tesla device, and Cutter explains to him not only how it should work as a magical prop, but also the particular significance this tank had for the two magicians. This exchange returns the narrative of the film to an earlier incident, the one in which Angier's wife is killed, which leads to the beginning of the feud.

Although film shorthand is an admirable thing, and modern audiences are as adept with it as most film-makers, it is not always the best.

There is no way an English judge would ever be able to spend time alone with a witness in the middle of a trial, or to examine evidential 'exhibits' in the alleged crime. In a real criminal hearing, all exhibits have to be brought into open court to be described by witnesses and to be examined by the jury, and if they're too big or too cumbersome, as they are in Borden's trial, then the court has to go to them.

In the case of Borden's murder trial, if the case left the courtroom the judge would have had to take with him both the defence and prosecution teams, the jury, the shorthand writer, the defendant and (because the defendant is a tricky customer who has been produced from prison) at least two of the jailers to keep him restrained. For the film-maker this would have created a cumbersome, crowded scene, one that might be difficult to shoot?

You can see the temptations of filmic shorthand to which Nolan succumbed – how much easier it was instead to have the brief expository dialogue between Cutter and the judge. In the context of the whole film it is an undeniably minor scene, of no greater importance than its use to establish the two plot elements.

However, as a writer I have discovered that fantasy, or the fantastic in general, gains a certain extra edge when it is placed in a context of testable reality. To take this shortcut against long-established juridical practice makes the scene unconvincing to anyone who has been involved with an important court case (and what is more important than a murder trial?).

Wouldn't it have been better to have made the warehouse scene one of crowding and confusion, Borden thought to be about to do one of his famous vanishing tricks and therefore making the warders nervous, the jurors and everyone else milling curiously around Cutter's precious apparatus, peering into it, prodding at it, while he tries to protect its secrets while having to explain them to the lawyers? It would have been reminiscent of the existing scenes in the film – there are at least two – in which we see members of the audience invited on to the stage to have a close look at the apparatus.

I believe Nolan took an easy way out, and lost the possibility of a realistic but also potentially dramatic, relevant and even amusing scene.

And as for the judge saying anachronistically of the apparatus, '*I'm sure beneath its bells and whistles it's got a simple and disappointing trick*' ... this is probably the worst line of dialogue in the film.

The phrase 'bells and whistles' aside, it makes a wrong assumption. One of the central maxims of stage magicians is the apparent paradox that intelligent observers – professional men and women, scientists, lawyers, journalists, judges, and so on – are amongst the *easiest* to deceive with conjuring tricks. (Children are the hardest, as a matter of fact known ruefully to every magician who has given a show to kids.)

A criminal judge being shown an illusionist's apparatus would make the opposite assumption to the one he is given to express here. As a professional observer, a man used to judgements, he would almost certainly assume that Tesla's scientific apparatus is fiendishly complicated, which is exactly what Cutter is trying to tell him. He would not leap to the assumption that the trick was '*simple and disappointing*'.

And '*bells and whistles*'? That's an indisputably modern coinage, often used in the worlds of software or electronic technology. It means extra features or frills that have been added to make something seem more attractive, without making it actually do more. To put that phrase in the mouth of a judge in Edwardian England is just plain silly.

It was not in the novel.

About one hour into the story the film contains one of its most intriguing and entertaining sequences.

Angier, in his desperation to emulate Borden's superior command of stage magic, has employed an out-of-work actor called Root, who bears a startling resemblance to himself. Naturally, Root is also played by Hugh Jackman, apparently relishing the opportunity to play broad comedy for a few minutes.

Root is a drunkard and has a loose tongue, constantly endangering the confidentiality of Angier's act, but his imposture is good and he is able to perform well on stage.

We see Angier and his crew building and rehearsing a complicated stage illusion, which involves two doors edge-on to the theatre audience, one on each side of the stage. Angier walks through one of them, but slips through a trapdoor and falls to the sub-stage level. In the same instant, Root rises from sub-stage on an elevator, and seems to appear suddenly at the second door. As Angier disappears behind the first door he tosses his top hat into the air and across the stage – as Root appears at the second door, he catches the hat, puts it on his head and takes the bow.

The scene is one of the two or three occasions in the film in which we see a whole illusion performed in front of the camera, from start to end. In this case it is all apparently shot in a continuous take from a static camera positioned with the theatre audience. We see the action as I have just described it, with no discernable joins or camera trickery. Angier steps from one side of the stage to the other in a fraction of a second.

For this brief episode, in an interesting way, the audience in the theatre is in exactly the same position as the audience of the film.

Within the fiction of the film the *theatre* audience knows, like all audiences of magic shows, that what they are seeing is a trick, even if they can't work out how it is done.

Within filmic grammar, the *film* audience also knows that it is a trick, but additionally has been fully informed in advance about the secret of the trick. We have seen the arrangement of trapdoors, an elevator, we know that Angier is using a twin double, we have seen them rehearsing.

Even so, when the trick is performed in the film, we are left not entirely sure how Nolan and his technical advisers (Ricky Jay and Michael Weber) pulled it off when they staged it. 'Root' might be Angier's double, but only one actor plays them both!

Sequences like this give the film of *The Prestige* a genuine sense of depth, a confirmation that the film makers were engaging intelligently with the multi-layered material of illusion and reality.

Firstly, by showing us the mechanical workings of the illusion the film underlines the maxim of all real magicians – that it is not the secrets of magic as such which create a brilliant illusion, but the skill of the performance.

Secondly, by presenting the scene from the apparently guileless one-position, one-take camera situated in the auditorium, they are putting the film audience in the same position as the theatre audience.

Thirdly, by use of unannounced and unrevealed cinematic tricks (was the shot doctored with computer software?, did Nolan's photographers use some kind of double exposure?, could Nolan have been using an uncredited real double to stand in for Hugh Jackman's alleged double?), the film performs its own magic.

However, as always we have to move on. The momentum of the film sweeps us from this sequence, one of the finest scenes in the whole film, to the next, which is not.

Angier is forced to realize that his trick is an inferior imitation of Borden's original. At the end of each performance he ends up out of sight beneath the stage, while Root glories in the spotlight and takes the applause. Also, the whole arrangement with Root is so full of risks he feels he must get rid of the unreliable ham actor and discover Borden's secret instead.

There is an exchange of dialogue between Angier and Olivia Wenscombe (played by Scarlett Johansson). Olivia is Angier's new stage assistant. She has also become his lover.

Angier tells Olivia he wants her to go to Borden, infiltrate his workshop and rehearsals, and act as his spy.

In both the novel and the film this is a crucial turn in the story. It is what screen-writing guru Syd Field calls a *Plot Point*: 'any incident, episode, or event that "hooks" into the action and spins it into another direction.'

Once Olivia has gone over to Borden's camp (because when she meets Borden she betrays Angier, almost from the start) the fate of both men is sealed and the conclusion of the story is inevitable.

Two unconvincing scenes ensue. The first is the one in which Angier puts the proposition to Olivia; the second is where she carries it out. In both scenes you can almost feel the actors straining to give credibility to the dialogue.

Olivia cannot understand why her new lover, and employer, should send her on this mission. Why is the secret so important to him? And why should Angier put his whole career in the hands of an assistant he has known for only a short time? The same is true in the following scene between Borden and Olivia – again, the actors do what they can, but the psychology is all wrong. Surely Olivia isn't so pliable that she would throw away her relationship with one man to extract a secret from another? Why should Borden trust her? He says he doesn't trust her, but even so he and Olivia soon fall in love.

The same sequence of events takes place in the novel: Olivia goes to spy on Borden on behalf of Angier, but ends up betraying Angier. However, the motivation is reversed.

In the book, the general situation is different. Angier and Olivia have been together for some years when this happens. The appointment of Root as Angier's stage double has had a disruptive effect on both their lives. Angier has suspicions about Root and Olivia getting interested in each other. He challenges Olivia about this, and she admits that some of the charm has gone out of their relationship. She tells Angier that his obsession with secrecy, and with Borden's secret in particular, is destroying not only him but her too. In an attempt to put things right, Olivia herself proposes that she should try to discover Borden's secret.

In plot terms, and eventually in the outcome, this is much the same, and perhaps it's a mistake to labour the point too much. However, I believe that this is more psychologically plausible than the film's idea of Olivia throwing everything away in her insecure life, just to serve her master. Neither Angier nor Borden is a particularly attractive character, in book or film, but the idea was that you should at least understand why they do what they do, even if you don't like them for it.

The first time I viewed the film everything about this sequence seemed false, unconvincing and unlikeable, and for a time I felt that it threatened to break the back of the story. Angier seemed so cold and calculating, Olivia so unbelievably manipulable, Borden so ready to take advantage of both the woman and Angier's cupidity. However, the brisk and compelling nature of the film's narrative intrigue soon moved events on.

For example, between the two dialogue scenes (Angier and Olivia, then Olivia and Borden) there is a flash forward to a visually arresting scene in which Tesla spectacularly fails to impress Angier with his newly built device. I think that by dropping this scene in between the two Olivia scenes the weakness in the Nolans' script was saved by sheer directorial or editorial panache. In all fairness the dashing style of film-making could have been used to try to disguise many more mistakes, but in fact Nolan does not have to. The rest of the story is tightly constructed, intelligently thought out and well told.

19. The End (part ii)

At the heart of *The Prestige* there lies a mystery.

Since it is a mystery I created myself I feel free to discuss it openly, especially with respect to how that mystery was treated in the film version of the novel. There might be some readers of this book who have neither read the novel nor seen the film, and who wish to enjoy discovering these things for themselves – to them I simply say: look away now, and thanks for staying with me until almost the end.

The rest of this book makes no attempt to preserve the plot matters which are contained within the story of both the film and the novel, and which are only revealed towards the end.

At the heart of *The Prestige* there lies a mystery.

As it is a novel and a film about illusions, there should be no surprise about this. Mystery was always intrinsic to the story, from the very first day I began working on the novel. One of the magicians was going to create and maintain an obsessive secret that would dominate his life. The anecdote about Ching Ling Foo creates this leitmotif.

The main problem with which this mystery presented me, while writing the novel, was how I should elucidate it. Short of thinking up a secret of such stunning originality, so surprising, original, new and unexpected that every reader would be dazzled by it, the mystery and the way it would be revealed to the reader had to be planned carefully. Most magical secrets are trivial, and revealing them generally has a bathetic effect.

In any event, I did not have, nor did I wish to have, an amazing concept that had never before been imagined. I wanted the secret to be a small one, a familiar one, a simple one. That is how magic itself works: the best tricks are achieved with the simplest methods.

For example, the rabbit that is produced from a hat is normally concealed inside a small bag hanging from a hook on the hidden side of the magician's table. The bag itself is made of the same material as the lining of the hat, so it becomes undetectable when placed inside the hat. Magicians use rabbits for their tricks because a tame rabbit, when put into a small, dark, confined space, stays still and silent. (A dove does the same, which is why this beautiful bird is also used in illusions.) Other animals when confined will inconveniently mew, bark, hiss, squawk or put up a bit of a struggle, but a rabbit can be trusted to wait quietly and in stillness. When the conjuror shows the audience that the hat is empty, it *is* empty, but when he picks it up a second time to perform his trick, he also unhooks the little bag and the rabbit swings swiftly into the hat, ready for the production.

Nothing could be simpler – but few tricks are as effective as THE RABBIT FROM THE HAT, a great and endlessly popular classic of conjuring.

The same principle of simplicity holds with even the grandest of illusions. There are wires invisible to the audience holding things in the air, the magician has assistants who dress in black and cannot be seen when they move on a suitably lit stage against a dark background, there are mirrors placed at an angle as *trompes l'oeils*, the ordinary-looking playing cards have secret marks on the back.

There are dozens of similar techniques, all simple, all effective. Most of them are so elementary that many people frankly disbelieve them, if all is explained. The wish for magic to be grand and mysterious affects most people.

I knew the mystery in my novel had to be just as simple and effective. I decided from the outset to make one of my 19th century magicians not one man, but two. Alfred Borden (in the film, Christian Bale) would in reality be a pair of identical twins: *Al*bert and *Fred*erick *Borden*. At an early stage in their lives the twins learned how easily other people mistake one of them for the other. As they grew up and discovered their interest in magic, they decided to use their identical appearance as a long-term stratagem of deception.

Entering manhood they established a pattern of living with which they were destined to continue for the remainder of their lives. They would divide normal life in two. One of them would live openly and publicly, calling himself Alfred Borden. The other would stay out of sight, living at a secret address. From time to time, pre-arranged, they would switch places: the hidden one would emerge and take over the part of Alfred Borden, while his brother would retreat into the shadows. Neither of them would be the 'real' Alfred Borden – they both were.

As their lives went on they developed an illusion that could be performed on stage, in which 'Alfred Borden' seemed to dematerialize and reappear somewhere else in a fraction of a second. The trick looked good, but for the brothers it enabled a hidden *Prestige*. With the working of the illusion they switched roles and identities. Whichever one of them took the applause at the end of the show became the

Alfred Borden who left the theatre openly and moved publicly in the world ... until the next time the illusion was performed.

As their popular success grew they performed their illusion more often. With the increased frequency the constant switching of roles meant that their dual identities tended to merge: they both thought of themselves as 'Alfred Borden'.

This imposture presented me, as novelist, with several problems of narration and structure, most of them trivial, some complicated.

The main problem, though, was the general one. How should the mystery be concealed from the readers at first, and then how could it be revealed as the book went on?

The trouble with a surprise revelation is pretty obvious. The fact that 'Borden' is actually a pair of twins is not difficult to guess. If the novelist or film-maker conceals it for too long, any reader who has worked it out will have seen it coming and might imagine from that point that there's no reason to continue reading. Others who don't spot the secret might well be jolted by the twist revelation at the end. Of those who are jolted, about half will be pleasantly surprised and perhaps delighted, but the other half will groan aloud and think, 'Is that *all* it was? They were twins! I've read three hundred pages to find out they were just twins!' (And so on.)

So I decided from the start that I would not make a secret of it, but instead create a mystery about Borden in which the readers would become interested, then involved, and finally be able to work it out for themselves. I assumed most people would do so long before the end of the story. That way, they would accept the information as part of the material in the novel and not as a big puzzle they have succeeded in solving. I also intended that if they should fail to pick up the clues, it shouldn't affect their reading of the novel.

The clues are not blatantly obvious, but they are there to be found.

For instance, in the opening section of the novel, which is the present-day story of the young journalist Andrew Westley, we discover that he has spent most of his life convinced that he has a twin brother from whom he has been separated. Twins are openly discussed. We also learn that Westley is a member of the Borden family and in fact a direct descendant of Alfred Borden's (giving birth to twins is an inherited trait).

In the long second part of the novel, Borden writes an account of his life, his career and the dispute with Angier. At first we think the narrative is being written by only one person, but not many pages into it there is an interruption. The narrator appears to be quarrelling with himself. An attentive reader might discern that there is a slight difference of writing style, as if someone else has taken over for a few pages. The word 'I' is used in an ambiguous way – sometimes it seems to mean 'you' or even 'we'. Later still we discover that Borden and his wife have twin children (giving birth to twins is an inherited trait).

There are other lesser clues in the book (the two apprentices in the wheelwright's workshop, the ease with which a performing magician spots Borden's unique nature), but the two examples I have singled out are the ones I intended the reader should think about, learning them from Borden's own account.

Later in the novel we read Rupert Angier's diary – this is the long fourth part. Angier constantly questions whether or not Borden is a twin, or if he is using some other kind of physical double. It is a matter of intense speculation for Angier and the subject is openly discussed.

For instance, Harry Cutter tells Angier that Borden is using a stage double – he must be, it is beyond a shadow of a doubt. As a magical specialist he discerns the method simply from Angier's description of what he has seen Borden doing on stage. Later, when he has seen Borden's performance for himself, Cutter amends this to the *certain* knowledge that he is using an identical twin. He tells Angier in a factual and unarguable way.

Angier accepts Cutter's explanation and believes it. But shortly afterwards a journalist approaches him and reverses everything.

The journalist (named 'Koenig' in the novel – he does not appear in the film) tells Angier that he too believed Borden to be a pair of identical twins, but that he has been conducting detailed investigative research into Borden's past. He has turned up Borden's birth record, family photographs, and so on. The conclusion he has drawn is that Borden *did not have an identical brother*, nor was there any other sibling who might have been used as a physical double.

Koenig gives Angier some written clues and references, so that he can satisfy himself about the facts.

Once again, Angier is thrown into a state of doubt. Later, he follows up Koenig's leads, and satisfies himself from what he assumes to be independent evidence that Borden was not and could not ever have been a twin. The mystery, as far as Angier is concerned, therefore remains, but perhaps by this time the reader would be starting to form an opinion too?

Some ten years later, Koenig returns to Angier to say that his earlier information was incorrect after all, that his inexperience as a young journalist had led him to being deceived. He is now satisfied that Angier had been right in the first place, that Borden is in fact two people, two brothers, identical twins. Koenig reveals that the earlier evidence he relied on had been falsified, presumably by the Borden brothers, as yet another manifestation of their obsessive secrecy and thoroughness.

Again, Angier accepts this information as being true, although by this point in the story it hardly matters any more.

By the end of the novel, when one of the Borden twins has died (although there is some question even about this, concerning the whereabouts of the body), and the other Borden is continuing to perform on stage (no longer including his 'transported man' illusion, which of course requires both brothers to be alive and well), the reader should be in no doubt about the truth.

Christopher Nolan, however, treated the Borden twins in a significantly different way, and as a result brought the film to a different conclusion.

One of the serious problems created by his double life concerns Borden's family.

A married man with children, Borden maintains a façade of outward normality, with a family, a house, servants, position in society, and so on. Meanwhile, his other self lives at the secret address, and from the middle of 1898 the twins have Olivia Wenscombe permanently installed in the apartment as their/his mistress. This rather modern arrangement would have been scandalous in the *fin de siècle* period, lending an extra edge of necessity to the secrecy.

But which of the two twins was the family man, which of them had the mistress?

To me, the inescapable answer was that the joint Alfred Bordens – obsessive controllers and completists – would have extended the deception into their private lives. Borden failed to tell the truth to the woman with whom he was in love. On the day the wedding took place, it perhaps was irrelevant to the twins which of the two of them actually went through the ceremony. Later, when Sarah, his wife, became pregnant, the twins would have again found it of no importance which of them it was who had inseminated her.

Maybe it was of no importance to him, or them, but what of Sarah's feelings? She would certainly have a view on the subject if she knew. And did she know?

Her knowledge, or otherwise, was a crucial matter. No one knows a man better than his wife. If the twins were swapping around, taking it in turns to play the role of husband and father, Sarah would soon realize something was going on. Even if she was not able to put it in so many words, she would know on some unconscious level. Borden was with his wife every day, deceiving her constantly.

Would she have worked it out?

Of course she would, and probably in exact detail.

But in knowing or realizing the deception, what would she do about it? She had a few choices.

She could have challenged Borden. She could have demanded he and his brother stop doing whatever it was they were doing. She could have run away from the marriage. She could have pretended it wasn't really happening and therefore didn't matter. Or she could have fully understood what was going on and why, but deliberately did nothing because of fear of the consequences for her and the children if the *status quo ante* was disrupted.

I thought the last was most likely. In my novel, Sarah made the difficult decision that it was in her best overall interests not to try to change anything. An arguable proposition, but I felt within the terms of the novel it was workable.

The same situation crops up in Christopher Nolan's film, but there is an essential difference.

The secret of Borden's double life is not going to be revealed until the very end, so for most of the film the audience is expected to assume that he is but one man. This one man first meets and courts Sarah (played by Rebecca Hall), then they marry. They have at least one child, Jess (played by Samantha Mahurin).

Jess, incidentally, is the child seen at the beginning of the film, when Cutter is performing a trick with a canary.

After Olivia Wenscombe enters Borden's life he becomes a darker, more devious figure, and Sarah is clearly suspicious of him. Christopher Nolan has the character say at the end of the film that only one of the two Borden twins actually met and wooed Sarah, and that he genuinely loves her. The other twin, sharing Sarah's life fifty per cent of the time, is part of the arrangement but he is always in a sense emotionally left out of it. This second twin feels free to start up a relationship with the beautiful and unattached Olivia.

However, that undoubtedly throws a shadow across the character of Borden in the film, because the pretence is maintained by the director, until the final scene, that Borden is but one man. Borden maintains unconvincingly that he totally loves both Olivia and Sarah, a duality that for the time being has to remain unexplained, as far as the film's audience is concerned. Sarah challenges him in separate scenes, saying that sometimes he seems genuinely to love her, sometimes not. She claims his feelings change from day to day.

Audiences seeing the film for a second time would probably pick up the intended irony here, but unless you know about his double life Borden comes across as insincere, conniving, lying to his wife, while

131

simultaneously conducting an affair with the glamorous Olivia. In the novel he is doing the same, but it is in a more unusual way. It does not make it more defensible, but the complexity of his deception rather circumvents normal morality.

The truth is of course that in the film we are seeing the effect of the dual life: Nolan is saying that one of the two brothers is in love with Olivia, while the other is genuinely and exclusively in love with Sarah. They continue to swap roles, as they have to, but it means for half the time they are with a woman they do not truly love. If the audience knows or realizes what is going on – such as if they should see the film for a second time – these scenes seem contrived, simplistic.

They lead to tragedy, Sarah is driven *in extremis* to killing herself without ever discovering the truth.

In the novel Sarah's fate is undescribed. The reader is not told how much she knew or discovered about her deceptive husband, but should realize from her actions that she must have made an accommodation with the unpleasant situation, probably for the sake of her children and for social appearances.

Had Nolan treated Borden's double identity as less of a secret, and given the audience more clues, I believe the scenes with Sarah would have taken on a fascinating and tragic quality. A challenge to the scriptwriters and the director, perhaps to the actors too, but it would have given Borden's character depth and consistency. He would not become more likeable, but at least his motives would be comprehensible. And the women, Sarah in particular, would have gained in stature as original and subtle characters.

Nolan, though, opted for concealment. He took the mystery from the novel and converted it into a secret. We are not intended to realize what is going on until it is explained at the end.

So we come to the conclusion of the film, with Christopher Nolan's two main secrets intact.

Borden (one of the brothers) is in prison waiting to be hanged for the murder of Robert Angier. Angier, in his true identity as Lord Caldlow, visits him. Borden, until this moment believing that he had been somehow responsible for Angier's death, because he had been present at the drowning, realizes when he sees Angier that he has been tricked and is about to be hanged for something he did not do. Although he passionately protests his innocence the execution goes ahead.

We cut straight from there to the basement of the theatre Angier has taken over, for use as a workshop-cum-storage depot. This is immediately after the execution.

A rubber ball bounces towards Angier, and as he looks up in surprise a shot rings out. He falls to his knees, fatally wounded. The man who has shot him is Borden (the other one of the brothers), and the scene is set for revelations. Borden has much to reveal to Angier; Angier too has some explaining to do.

While the plot of the film is tightly constructed, with no loose ends that are easily detectable – this tautness of story, after so much multi-layered complexity, is a genuine achievement by the Nolans – the staging of the conclusion is unsatisfactory.

Borden, apparently miraculously unhurt by the hanging we have just witnessed, and Angier, in his last moments of life, at last do what perhaps they should have done all along, and own up to each other.

This is a conventional ending to a mystery, comparable perhaps to the type of murder mystery where the great detective gathers the suspects in one room and after explaining the method to everyone points the finger at the culprit. Given the unoriginality of the set-up, Nolan conducts it reasonably well. Christian Bale in particular acts the scene plausibly and with conviction, and the illustrative cutaways are short, shocking and cruelly effective.

Borden explains his secret, and the identity of the enigmatic 'Fallon' is at last revealed. One of the central mysteries of the film is revealed in a shot that is not for the squeamish.

An unusual aspect of the long final scene is that

much of it is difficult to hear and follow. This is surprising in a film where so much attention has been lavished on technical details, but the sound mix is poor.

The 'deathbed' confessional exchange between Borden and Angier is conducted in a series of hoarse whispers and unclear croaks that are close to unintelligible. With my special knowledge of the story I was able to guess what they were saying on a first hearing, but I certainly missed about half of the exact words. On second and subsequent viewings I found the same, so it was not a question of poor sound equipment in the first cinema (nor does it seem likely to be the failure of my own hearing). With the DVD and a copy of the script I have subsequently deciphered the whole sequence, but of course I wonder about the effect this poor recording quality has on members of audiences not concerned to pay the same close attention.

For instance, after Borden has shot him and is standing before him, Angier realizes that the man he sees *cannot* be the same man whom we have just seen being hanged. Enlightenment dawns in his face.

He says hoarsely, '*A brother, a twin.*' Then: '*You were Fallon the whole time.*'

Hugh Jackman's articulation is not clear: the annoying modern fad for extreme close-up whispers in some scenes is playing against the actors here. This is perhaps the key revelation of the film story, and does not in any way confirm what the audience might be expected to know. It is the disclosure of the one mystery that is so far unexplained, but it's hard to be sure what Angier has said with those breathy words. Only in the first of several explicit cutaways, a few seconds later, when we see Borden/Fallon together, does it start to become clear what Angier has realized.

Later, the revelation is reversed: now it is Borden's turn to be enlightened. Angier tries to defend his extreme actions.

He croaks to Borden, '*Do you want to see what it cost me? You didn't see where you are, did you? Look, look!*'

Again, there was a problem with the actor's articulation. Only when I had a copy of the DVD with subtitles was I able to work out exactly what Angier said. His meaning of '*where you are*' means the presence of the many deep glass-sided water tanks, standing around the two men to create a ghoulish aisle. '*Look, look!*' This is hard to hear, so it is impossible to discern his meaning. Borden barely glances away from him in response, presumably taking in with a single glimpse the tanks and what they impend for him and the other man. Oddly, though, the audience is denied this knowledge, and the point is largely lost. Christopher Nolan is still holding back, concealing his final secret to the bitter end.

A similar lack of clarity occurs in Michael Caine's voice-over. Cutter is one of the most important characters in the film: to the end of the story he remains the still centre of sanity and calmness, caught in the middle of the deadly feud between the other two. Michael Caine plays Cutter with skill: whenever he is on the screen he dominates the action, and gives the audience a sense of understandable reality to hold on to, in spite of the various contradictions that seem to be occurring.

Michael Caine's opening voice-over – the *Pledge*, the *Turn*, the *Prestige* – is, as already noted, a tremendous way into the story. Nolan reprises this commentary at the end in a remarkably effective way.

The film concludes, as it begins, with (in effect) a main illusion being performed in counterpoint with a simple one.

Here, at the end, the main illusion is the revelation of what these two men have been doing to each other and their confessions about it – the simple one is a re-run of the trick with the canary, performed for the amusement of Jess, Borden's little daughter.

Cutter's voice is cued at exactly the right moment: Nolan's timing is perfect. It's a moment when you feel your skin tingle with anticipation. We are returning to the opening images, but now our knowledge of what is going on is almost, but not quite, complete.

And this time there is a difference in what Cutter is implying. With the words '*You have to bring it back*' Borden reappears in the room, to be reunited with his child. All this is powerful and moving in effect.

But as before, Cutter's narrative extends across non-linear time. Nolan's fascination with disjointed time continues, even in these climactic moments. The reunion with little Jess must be in the near future, after the deathbed scene, because again the time shifts.

Back in the old theatre, immediately after Angier's death from the gunshot (but before the reunion with Jess), Borden is wandering around in the basement where the glass-walled tanks are lined up, while the fire from Angier's overturned oil lamp spreads. Borden is stepping between the flames, looking at the tanks, trying to understand what they mean, but what the tanks contain is still not explicitly revealed to the audience. Even in these final few seconds of the film, Nolan is holding back his secret as long as possible.

Cutter says the words: '*Now you're looking for the secret. But you won't find it because, of course, you're not really looking. You don't really want to work it out. You want to be ... fooled.*'

Inexplicably, Michael Caine lowers his voice with the last word. While we strain to work out what he said, we are given about half a second to regard the secret, Nolan's final flourish, but then the screen goes black. It is a jolt into the same darkness that Borden himself evoked, with the opening words, '*Are you watching closely?*'

But this time the film has ended.

The film of *The Prestige* is an unusual and remarkable effort. It defies normal analysis. It has one of the most complicated and sophisticated narrative structures ever seen in an entertainment film. It makes intelligent demands on its audience, and rewards the attentive audience with a harvest of even more imaginative energy. It makes no concessions to expectability. It hints at events more than it shows them, but it frequently produces subtle and brilliant visual metaphors. Much of the dialogue is quiet, elliptical, conversational, under-stated. *The Prestige* has no precedents in mainstream cinema, except perhaps glimpses of what might come from Nolan's earlier films that we can discern with hindsight.

The photography throughout is beautiful and effective. The cinematographer, Wally Pfister, decided to mount many of the scenes with a hand-held camera – this is a radical departure from the more stately presentation we have grown used to seeing in other Victorian period pieces. Pfister's constantly twitching camera is under control: the movements are tiny and marginal, lending the film an almost subliminal undercurrent of modernity, nerviness, perhaps a documentary feel, as if the story was being captured by a freelance crew on assignment to cover the events as they happened. But the contrast between this superbly modern approach to photography and the lush costumes, the warm amber lighting of the interiors, the detailed dressing of the street scenes, the rococo flourishes of the theatrical interiors, is all part of the visual misdirection that Nolan's ensemble is creating. *The Prestige* looks like a period piece with twenty-first century touches – in fact it is of course a contemporary film, sharply modern, one that is set in an imagined past.

The two Academy Award nominations the film received – for cinematography, and for art direction – were incisively right. Naturally, I should have preferred more honours to be heaped on the film, but the two nominations it did receive were deserved. That other films collected the actual awards on the night says whatever we might agree it says about voters, or awards, or any kind of prize competition. But I do believe that these technical achievements for *The Prestige* were significant ones, and the photography and design compare in their individuality and sheer originality with the amazing script adaptation.

I feel differently about the sound quality. The

soundtrack should be remixed to make the dialogue more audible. So many crucial arguments or revelations are made in casual voices, sometimes even as asides, that important elements of the story can be misunderstood, or even missed altogether. *The Prestige* is a film driven by its plot, and significant moments in the plot are stated, not depicted. Informal, conversational style dialogue is attractive and naturalistic, but mumbling is always irritating.

Naturally, I will seem to have a preferential view of the film. I consider that it has actually been under-regarded so far, but time will tell. Its qualities easily outweigh the small deficiencies I have concentrated on, but they reveal themselves gradually. It is not a film for a single viewing – it rewards second and third times. In the future I believe it will come to be recognized as a great classic of cinema, standing comparison with many of the acknowledged masterpieces of the past. I can make these large claims because, as must be clear by now, I had almost nothing at all to do with making the film. The book is mine; the film is theirs.

The Prestige will probably not been seen again in cinemas, except in revivals or at festivals. Its future is in the DVD version, in the television re-runs, in whatever technical innovation comes along in the future to enable people to watch movies in their homes. Like all films it recedes into the collective memory of past movies, leaving behind whatever impression it made on each of us.

Some I know have disliked the film – many more have admired and enjoyed it. A few have been baffled by its complexities and layers, its understated ideas and reversals, while most audiences have found it stimulating, challenging, tantalizing, an experience to be repeated. But not, in spite of Harry Cutter's last words, an exercise in being fooled. It is all too subtle for that.

Appendix - The Mystery

When you look closely at a film, as I have done with *The Prestige*, you become aware of the sometimes uncanny relationship between practical film-making technique and the subject matter of the film itself.

The Prestige is a story about doubles, twins, doppelgängers, illusion, mistaken identity, concealment, legerdemain, sleight of hand. Christopher Nolan himself has said (e.g., in the accompanying material on the DVD) that from the outset he saw parallels between stage magic and film-making.

Nothing you see in any film is of course real: it is stating the obvious to point out that actors play the parts and say the lines written by others, sets are designed and built, special effects are used to create explosions and floods, stunt men perform the risky stuff, extras play the crowds and passers-by, doubles do the swimming, the nude scenes, the horse-riding, and so on.

A magician's act creates a similar false reality.

Everything is prepared or crafted. A cabinet is shown to be empty, when of course it cannot be. A saw that is about to slice an assistant in half is demonstrated as a real one, when of course it could not be. A deck of cards is shown to be untampered-with, when naturally the trick would not work unless the cards had been tampered with. Nothing is real or what it seems, or even (and this is what magicians call misdirection) what the audience is encouraged to assume is real or reliable.

The little mystery concerning the character 'Fallon' in *The Prestige* deserves a footnote, even though I imagine it could be solved by speaking to anyone who was on the production crew of the film.

Fallon does not exist in the novel. In the film he is a mysterious, silent presence in several of the scenes concerning Borden. We first see him standing in the public gallery of the courtroom where Borden is on trial, holding hands with Borden's daughter Jess. A silent signal passes between Borden and Jess, after which Fallon leads the little girl from the court.

We do not get a close look at Fallon's face until close to the end of the film, but he appears so frequently that it's possible to recognize him. He has a fattish face, wears moon-round spectacles, has thick hair and a bushy moustache. He has a rotund figure. He never speaks, although Borden addresses him from time to time. We learn that Fallon is Borden's *ingénieur*, and at one point Borden calls him 'Bernard'.

Something is clearly odd about Fallon, even if you are seeing the film for the first time and have not been told what the film is about. His weird appearance, his habitual silence, his inexplicably close relationship with Borden's family, all draw attention to him. You suspect, perhaps, that it is one of the other characters in disguise, but the actor's make-up is good and it's not a simple matter to identify him.

In the final sequence of the film Borden reveals that 'Fallon' is in fact himself, or his twin brother, in disguise. We get a good look at Fallon's face for the first time, and at last we see unarguably that Christian Bale is visible beneath the disguise. This revelation comes as a considerable surprise to many people, but it's also fair to say that a good number of people have inevitably seen through the disguise before this moment. Much excited discussion has gone on in the blogs about *The Prestige*.

To take the matter beyond dispute, or so one would think, Nolan gives us a cutaway to shots of the two brothers, both of course played by Christian Bale, taking off or putting on the Fallon disguise. It's an effective moment.

In these days of computer-enhanced imagery, it is no longer an inexplicable novelty for a cinema audience to see two Christian Bales side by side in the same shot. (There are similar moments in the Angier/Root sequence.) But in at least one scene in the film, where Borden and Fallon turn up together at a restaurant, the visual context does not appear to allow for CGI techniques – a tracking camera shot as Borden, Olivia and Fallon walk between the tables, with several other people present in the same shot. Almost immediately 'Fallon' covers his face with his hand as he walks closer to the camera, suggesting that it is not Christian Bale in disguise, patched in later by a computer.

Also, in the production video on the DVD, presumably made without a CGI budget, Borden and Fallon appear together in at least two off-guard shots, preparing the next scene with the director and cameraman.

True to the general deviousness of the plot of *The Prestige*, it seems that a double was used to play the double. No actor is credited with the part of Fallon, although all films use stand-ins and stunt doubles. The difference here is that the double is a significant part of the plot, seen in many different scenes.

Who was it? The credits are silent. Not even a spurious 'Alec Cawthorne', who played a similar role in the 1972 release of *Sleuth*. Nor an 'Alan Smithee', taking a break from his directorial duties.

A small thing for a director to use a stand-in, but in this film, in *this* part? Wheels within wheels, indeed.

Notes

1. The End (part i)
[1] The Internet Movie Database carries many lists of 'best' and 'worst' movies, which can be treated with whatever seriousness is felt appropriate. The main list quoted here, however, appears to be responsibly managed, with the people who take part in the voting having to satisfy certain criteria of dedication to film. The mathematical formula by which the list is compiled is also described:

weighted rating (WR) $= (v \div (v+m)) \times R + (m \div (v+m)) \times C$

where:
R = *average for the movie (mean)* = *(Rating)*
v = *number of votes for the movie* = *(votes)*
m = *minimum votes required to be listed in the Top 250 (currently 1300)*
C = *the mean vote across the whole report (currently 6.7)*

Positions on the list change only slowly, and only a

small percentage of newly released films make it on to the list, or once there remain in place. *The Prestige* has been slowly ascending the list since it was first released.

The IMDb website is located at:
http://www.imdb.com/chart/top?tt0482571

2. **The Thought**

[2] Here is the way the six principles of magic are set out in the novel:

1. Production: *the magical creation of somebody or something out of nothing,*

2. Disappearance: *the magical vanishing of somebody or something into nothing,*

3. Transformation: *the apparent changing of one thing into another,*

4. Transposition: *the apparent changing of place of two or more objects,*

5. Defiance of Natural Laws: *for example, seeming to defeat gravity, making one solid object appear to pass through another, producing a large number of objects or people from a source apparently too small to have held them, and*

6. Secret Motive Power: *causing objects to appear to move of their own will, such as making a chosen playing card rise mysteriously out of the pack.*

3. **The Writing**

[3] The anecdote about Ching Ling Foo is still in the novel, near the beginning. It's a key passage in the book, the rationale for almost everything that follows.

The story of Ching also crops up in the movie, re-created rather impressively I thought. For me, seeing the actor who played Ching actually perform his most famous illusion was one of the high points of the film. (From a glimpse of the preparations in the 'making-of' feature on the DVD, it looks as if the actor was not using Ching's unique method.) Just as impressive was the scene that followed, in which Hugh Jackman bravely tried to reproduce the same trick.

There's a small mistake in the movie: the script calls the Chinese magician *Chung Ling Soo*, as do the film's credits. They have muddled him up with another magician, a white American who disguised himself as Chinese, modelled himself on Mr Ching, and who later notoriously died performing the dangerous bullet-catching trick. That, however, is another story, although 'Soo' and Foo did, coincidentally, feud with each other in a way remarkably similar to Borden and Angier. Feuds between magicians were more common than not, such is the nature of the work and the kind of personality drawn to performance magic.

But how ironic is it that people making a film about magicians feuding and using doubles should make this elementary mistake?

[4] One of the illusionists I interviewed, by then retired from

performing, asked to be kept anonymous. The other was John Wade, a British magician recommended to me by the Magic Circle. I feel indebted to both these men, who gave me a lot of time and helped me in many small ways, particularly with insights into the mentality of a magician setting out to create or build an illusion. I gave Mr Wade a credit in the first UK and US editions of the novel, but his name appears to have been dropped from later editions.

Will Goldston's book, reprinted in an American facsimile edition, became the model for the book which Andrew Westley is sent in the first few pages of *The Prestige*. Although I did not use it immediately, Goldston's book became invaluable in a later draft of the novel. Then I semi-disguised Goldston's book by replacing his padlock with mention of an oath that had to be sworn by the original purchaser of the book.

Anecdotally, a certain real mystery surrounds the way in which I acquired my copy of this book.

Walking to the post office one morning, I noticed that one of the local shops which had been empty for some time had been reopened. It was now a magic shop. As I was just then working on the draft of the opening pages of *The Prestige* I thought this fortuitous, to say the least. Of course, I went inside without a second thought. The interior of the shop was a bit rough-and-ready, scented with incense and specializing in robes and ritual apparatus, but there were two glass cases displaying proprietary tricks. Most of these would be familiar from any magic catalogue, and can be found in magic box-sets sold to children. Disappointed,

I headed for the door.

The old-hippie proprietor, sitting behind the counter, asked me if I had been looking for anything in particular. I guardedly told him I was a writer and was trying to research stage illusions. He reached under the counter and produced four books, on the top of which was the Goldston title. As soon as I realized what it was (I had heard of it, but had never seen a copy before) I knew I had to have it. The man wanted £5 for it, which I thought was a bargain.

A fairly common feature of ghost or supernatural stories is the narrator's surprise discovery of a dark backstreet shop with dusty windows, selling magical or supernatural apparatus, which has later inexplicably disappeared when he tries to find it again. After the time I went inside, I passed my local magic shop almost every day but I never saw it open for business again. It was always unlit, the door was locked and there was a steadily growing pile of unopened mail visible on the floor inside the door. Soon all trace of the shop had vanished. At present the premises are being used as a hairdresser's salon.

The edition I bought was:

Exclusive Magical Secrets by Will Goldston; New York 1977; Dover Publications Inc.; ISBN: 0-486-23432-0.

[5] One of Tesla's public performances is re-created in Christopher Nolan's film.

Tesla mounts a demonstration at London's Albert Hall, and both Angier and Borden attend it. However, the show does not go ahead because Tesla too is involved in a bitter feud with a rival, in his case with Thomas Alva Edison. Edison has managed to get the display aborted on public safety grounds. Before the show ends, though, both Angier and Borden are able to take a good look at the terrifying effects of a Tesla coil.

The feud between Edison and Tesla is a matter of historical certainty, and from my point of view as novelist it enhanced the central theme of my novel, which was the endless rancour that can arise between competitors envious of each other's presumed success.

The special effects used in the movie to show the Tesla coil in operation are a wonder to behold. They are in fact better to look at than the real thing, which is more frightening than spectacular.

[6] The one significant difference between the film and the novel is that Christopher Nolan's film is set exclusively at the end of the 19th century, with no reference to the present day. In this, Nolan seemed to be concurring with a view several people had about the novel.

For instance, when the reviews of the novel appeared on first publication, the modern story was often referred to disparagingly as the 'frame', as if providing a context was all it was there to do. For the reasons I have given I disagree with this. The modern sequence is not the frame for the 'real' story in the 19th century; nor are the magicians' written accounts 'flashbacks' from the modern day. The novel is a whole, the context is the passage of time, the consequences are human.

Although I think Nolan's decision was a sensible and defensible one in cinematic terms, and one which perhaps if he had asked me in advance I should have agreed with or might even have suggested, the real problem is that his adaptation robs the story of its proper ending. The story of Borden and Angier ends where I placed it, in the last five pages or so of the novel. Nolan came up with a different climax.

The later chapters of this book deal with the Nolans' script adaptation and their revised ending of the story.

4. The Book

[7] This attractive but flawed edition, under the Touchstone imprint of Simon & Schuster UK, sold well in hardback, and within a year or two had gone out of print.

The price to book collectors settled down at around £20 for a clean copy, and it stayed unexcitingly in that region for several years. Since the release of the film, the price has rocketed. The last time I looked on *abebooks.com*, copies were being offered for $2,000. I have kept two mint-condition copies locked away, for my children to own one day. The book is dedicated to them, incidentally.

Link: http://www.abebooks.com/servlet/SearchRes ults?an=Christopher+Priest&sortby=1&tn=The+Prestige &x=51&y=16

11. The Batman

[8] After shooting of *The Illusionist* was complete, there was a surprisingly long period of silence. It was impossible to

find out when the film was likely to appear. The only source of information I came across was a fan website, which said that *The Illusionist* was still trying to find a distributor. It was screened at one or two film festivals, but no major distributor stepped forward.

Not long after *The Prestige* was announced, a release schedule for *The Illusionist* was suddenly published. It is hard to avoid the conclusion that when Nolan's project became known, someone decided to move quickly and get *The Illusionist* exhibited before *The Prestige* could be ready.

In the event, *The Illusionist* was given limited release in the USA in mid-August 2006, and full release on September 1, 2006. *The Prestige* was not released in the USA until October 20, 2006. I believe this had a noticeably negative effect on the way *The Prestige* was greeted – it was assumed by many commentators to be 'similar to' *The Illusionist*, or one of a perceived new genre of films about magic. In fact, the films are different in almost every way.

In the UK, the situation was reversed. *The Prestige* was released at the beginning of November 2006, but *The Illusionist* did not appear until three months later.

I could not help noticing that much of the negative comment in the US press about *The Prestige* turned up again in the British press, this time levelled at *The Illusionist*. Even experienced film critics love pointing out superficial similarities.

[9] If the IMDb poll I mentioned earlier has any relevance at

all, at the time of this writing *Batman Begins* is positioned many places below *The Prestige*, in the low 100s. *The Dark Knight*, Nolan's sequel to *Batman Begins*, went straight to No. 1 on its release in the summer of 2008, but has slipped slightly since.

Perhaps it's worth adding that *Memento* deservedly rides high in the 20s (and has been in the top 100 almost since its first release), while *Following* and *Insomnia* are not in the list at all.

13. The Screenplay

[10] The Nolans' adapted screenplay of *The Prestige* was passed over in the Academy Awards for the year 2006. It did not receive even a nomination in this category. Meanwhile the 'adapted screenplay' for *Borat* enjoyed a nomination. *Borat* was an amusing and enjoyable film, but much of it was improvised with hapless members of the public. The 'adaptation' as a screenplay consisted of a few TV sketches which had been converted for the film.

It seems to me the Academicians made a serious omission here: whatever anyone might think of *The Prestige* as a finished film, pro or con, the Nolans' script adaptation is a work of immense skill.

I say this unambiguously, feeling that if anyone in this world should know the quality of the achievement, it is me. There is hardly a line of dialogue or moment of action in the film that can be traced back word-for-word, yet the whole thing is faithful to the novel in spirit, in story and in effect. I have differences with the screenplay in places, but none of those detracts from my general impression that it is a classic film adaptation of an existing novel, one which intending screenwriters would do well to study alongside the novel. I have heard other people say that the Nolans' adaptation is one of the finest ever.

I assume that when deciding what to vote for, Academicians judge only what they rate as the quality of the finished product, and do not go back to the original source to examine what the adapter has actually done.

I also assume the omission was a disappointment to Jonathan Nolan at least, but this is another aspect of the film in which time will eventually tell. Nolan has probably shrugged off the incident. As noted above, writers should always move on from awards not won, unfavourable reviews received, poor distribution of books or films, and other disappointments outside their control.

Meanwhile, the winner of the Academy Award in the adapted screenplay category that year was William Monahan, for *The Departed*. This was adapted from an original script by Siu Fai Mak and Felix Chong for their 2002 Hong Kong film, *Infernal Affairs*.

14. **The Secrecy**

[11] A few of the IMDb forum participants seemed fairly well informed, stayed out of the more puerile speculations about Batman, etc., and one or two of them even appeared to have some genuine knowledge of the film world.

One day, one of these people asserted that the entire production of *The Prestige* had moved to Scotland, and was filming on location in Motherwell. The information was stated in terms of absolute certainty, and even when challenged by others the writer stoutly maintained that he had insider information.

Motherwell? A Hollywood production moving to Motherwell in the middle of a shoot? It defied belief. The only possible explanation, and that a remote one, might be that the film required some shots of Victorian buildings. My knowledge of Motherwell was tiny, but I supposed it was possible that this former industrial town might have some picturesque terraces or municipal buildings. Surely there were other places with the same heritage, less far from the beaten track?

I turned to the modern research tool, and Googled '*Motherwell Nolan Prestige*'. Anyone attempting the same search today will probably find similar results.

Motherwell boasts many businesses with 'Prestige' in the name: bridal cars, villas, shop fittings, mortgages, a funeral director, secondhand cars, a decoding operation, and an 'experience' (whatever that might be). Less predictably, there is or was a Councillor Nolan in Motherwell, and there had been a parliamentary candidate named Nolan in Motherwell.

But no film directors, no Hollywood production, no location shooting.

[12] Of these films, *The Sixth Sense*, *The Usual Suspects* and *Gambit* were based on 'original' scripts: that is, they were not adaptations.

Psycho, released in 1962, was based on a novel by Robert Bloch, first published in 1959.

Fight Club (1999), was based on Chuck Palahniuk's novel published in 1996.

Sleuth (1972, and remade in 2007) was based on Anthony Shaffer's stage play of the same name, first performed in 1970.

15. **The Veto**

[13] Many tie-in editions are in fact brought out specially – the producers provide the publishers with an early copy of the screenplay, a writer hurriedly 'novelizes' it and the book is rushed out in time to coincide with the release of the film.

Although most novelizations are written professionally, and within certain limitations they are written well, they are never as satisfactory as the real thing. I have written novelizations myself, and have always been acutely aware of the limitations. Film scripts are in their nature schematic and under-described, so the writer has the opportunity to flesh out the story with extra details. Indeed, the details *have* to be fleshed out, because most screenplays are only about 100 or 120 pages long, and there's a lot of white space. A typical novel manuscript will be at least 200 pages, and usually more. But padding can only be taken so far. How can you anticipate the extra details? To give some idea of the potential traps:

You usually don't know who the stars will be, and you definitely don't know who will be playing the minor characters. You have only the vaguest idea of settings. (A scene will often be described in the briefest possible way. For example, as: EXT. CITY STREET. DAY.) You probably know the period, the country and the type of story – thriller, comedy, science fiction, etc. – but you have no information about the pace, the costumes, the way the photography is going to be lit, the mood the music will induce. You can pick up hints all along, and make intelligent guesses, but some parts of a screenplay will always be unhelpful.

A good example is the treatment of love or sex scenes. Is the characters' lovemaking going to be explicit or implied? (Physical love is rarely described in a screenplay, and in most cases will simply say something like: 'Sebastian and Angela go to bed and make love.') If the novelizing author steps too far in one direction, the novel will seem coy when compared with the film; step too far the other way, and it will seem exploitative. An error in either direction might well arouse the wrath of the film-maker.

One novelization I wrote several years ago, from a fast-moving, literate and rather funny script, was criticized by the director as being 'not dark enough.' Such problems proliferate. What sort of car does the main character drive? A late model, an old jalopy, an off-road vehicle, a sports car? What's his/her fashion sense like? Are the characters old or young? What sort of accents do they have?

One of the films I novelized starred the English actor, Jude Law. It was an American film set in the USA. What sort of role was Mr Law playing? Presumably an American, but the screenplay didn't say. Was it more likely he would be playing an Englishman abroad? Or was this actor famous for his handsomely aristocratic Anglo looks going to put on an American accent? This might sound like too much worry about too small a detail, but when you're writing a novel you need all the help you can get.

And then there's the greatest limitation of all: a lack of time. A writer might be allowed only three or four weeks in which to produce the manuscript of a whole novel.

17. **The Release**

[14] In May 2008, during a visit to Yekaterinburg in the Urals, I went to a cinema showing of *The Prestige* dubbed into Russian. There were no English subtitles, of course, but my wife Leigh and I had little difficulty in following the story. It was a considerable novelty watching Michael Caine apparently speaking Russian. The Russians we were with said that the dubbing was in fact not all that good, but I was interested to see that the sound mix was much better than it was in English.

Index

Printed in the United Kingdom by
Lightning Source UK Ltd., Milton Keynes
141466UK00001B/3/P